Spiritual Reflections
on the Sunday Gospels, **Cycle B**

To
Praise,
To
Bless,
To
Preach

Peter John Cameron, O.P.

Our Sunday Visitor Publishing Division
Our Sunday Visitor, Inc.
Huntington, Indiana 46750

Nihil Obstat:

Francis J. McAree, S.T.D.
Censor Librorum

Imprimatur:

✠ Patrick J. Sheridan, D.D.,
Vicar General, Archdiocese of New York
March 16, 1999

Our Sunday Visitor Publishing Division
Our Sunday Visitor, Inc.
200 Noll Plaza
Huntington, IN 46750

ISBN: 087973-822-7
LCCN: 99-70508

Cover design by Rebecca Heaston
PRINTED IN THE UNITED STATES OF AMERICA
822

For my brothers and sisters with love:

Michael and Sally
Mark
Paul and Donna
Tim and Helen
Trisha and Paul
and
Nancy Leroy

TABLE OF CONTENTS

PART ONE: REFLECTIONS ON THE SUNDAY GOSPELS

PART TWO: REFLECTIONS ON SOLEMNITIES AND FEASTS THAT MAY FALL ON SUNDAY

PREFACE

"To Praise, To Bless, To Preach" is the motto of the Order of Preachers: the Dominicans. As the Dominican Constitutions assert, Dominicans give themselves "to the proclamation of the Word of God, preaching the Name of our Lord Jesus Christ throughout the world. . . . Thus preachers must first accept the whole Gospel and seek a living understanding of the mystery of salvation as it is handed down and explained by the Church." However, in a certain sense, this is the vocation of every Christian vis-à-vis the Word of God. To praise, to bless, and to preach is what the Gospel calls, enables, and empowers every believer to do.

As the *Catechism of the Catholic Church* (CCC) teaches us, praise is that form of prayer — that response to the Word of God — which recognizes most immediately that God is God. Praise lauds God for his own sake and glorifies him simply because HE IS (CCC 2639). Our prayerful reflection on the Gospel equips us to praise God as he deserves.

Similarly, the Word of God that blesses the human heart enables us to bless God in return as the source of every blessing (CCC 2645). Blessing is that encounter between God and his people in which God's gift and our acceptance of that gift become united in a sacred dialogue with each other (CCC 2626). The more we meditate on the Word of God, especially the Gospels, the more do we grow in that divine dialogue.

And finally, God gives us his word to preach. For those who are ordained, preaching takes a liturgical form: homilies, sermons, conferences, etc. The laity proclaim the Good News with the witness of their lives and via the personal opportunities for evangelization that every day affords. Accordingly, the Word of God remains one of the crucial sources for every Christian's life of prayer. In fact, the spiritual life itself is a kind of preaching, for Christian prayer is our speaking to God with the very Word of God (CCC 2769).

Please note that these reflections are not fully formed homilies meant to be preached. Rather, I look upon them as so many spiritual bouillon cubes ready to be added by the reader to the heated waters of the Spirit so as to make a satisfying evangelical soup.

I am especially grateful to the *National Catholic Register* for permission to reprint a number of reflections that first appeared in the *Register*.

As we reflect on the Good News, may our heartfelt love of the whole Gospel move us to praise, to bless, and to preach the salvation that Christ, the Word of God, unceasingly offers us in his Church.

Peter John Cameron, O.P.

INTRODUCTION

WHY IS PREACHING PART OF MASS?

In the introduction to his book *Christian Faith & The Theological Life*, the eminent theologian Romanus Cessario, O.P., states: "Jesus inaugurates the theological life through his preaching but especially by his salvific death" (p. 6). Accordingly, the Church recognizes an organic unity of preached word and paschal action in the liturgy. In that union, preaching finds its true liturgical home, and it answers the question: "Why is preaching part of the Eucharistic liturgy?"

WORD AS LITURGICAL FOUNDATION

The Eucharistic assembly of the faithful, which manifests the visible expression of the Church, was prefigured in the ministry of Jesus through the conjoining force of his preaching and teaching. Through his word and the sending out of his disciples, Jesus called all people to come together around him. The preaching of Jesus summoned innumerable individuals, formed them as the People of God, and inaugurated the Church.

In the faith-gatherings he convened, Christ preached in a way that manifested the mysteries of the Kingdom. His subsequent healings and miracles illustrated the deepest meaning of his preaching. Even in this proto-Eucharistic moment of salvation history we see the essence of a key liturgical principle at work:

> The liturgical word and action are inseparable both insofar as they are signs and instruction and insofar as they accomplish what they signify. When the Holy Spirit awakens faith, he not only gives an understanding of the Word of God, but through the sacraments also makes present the "wonders" of God which it proclaims (CCC 1155).

In this way, the salvific words of Jesus anticipated the power of his Paschal Mystery. Christ's words, along with all the mysteries of his life, serve as the foundations of what he goes on to dispense in the sacraments.

13

Jesus communicates this same dynamic to his apostles in sending them forth to preach the Gospel to every creature. For Jesus willed that the work of salvation which they preached be set in train through the sacraments around which the Church's liturgical life revolves. As a result, the liturgical work of the Church proceeds from the preaching of Christ's chosen ministers.

Such an insight strips away common misconceptions about the nature and purpose of liturgical preaching. For the Church defines preaching as the faithful preservation, elucidation, and propagation of the Word of God. The homily is an extension of the liturgical proclamation of Sacred Scripture; it is ontically united to the Word of God. As such, the homily acts as an exhortation that calls the faithful to accept the message they hear as God's authentic Word and to put it into practice. In short, the homily of the preacher is not essentially distinct from the Word of God proclaimed; rather, *authentic preaching continues that proclamation in another mode.*

Therefore, excluding the homily from the liturgy threatens to diminish the vivacity of the Word of God. The full proclamation of Sacred Scripture remains an integral part of sacramental celebrations. This truth compels preachers to realize the essential role preaching plays in predisposing God's people for the Church's sacramental life.

What began with the teaching of Jesus, and was furthered via the preaching of the apostles, perseveres today in the liturgical preaching of the Church. The economy of Revelation continues to be realized by words and deeds that remain intrinsically bound up with each other. Preached words persist in proclaiming divine works and illumining their inherent mystery. As the *Catechism* affirms: "The preaching of the Word is required for the sacramental ministry itself, since the sacraments are sacraments of faith, drawing their origin and nourishment from the Word" (CCC 1122).

St. Thomas Aquinas provides helpful insight as to how the sacraments draw their origin and nourishment from the Word. In considering the creation of the world, St. Thomas compares the action of the Word of God to the creative process of an artist. He notes that just as artists make everything from a model that they first design in their heart — their "word" — so does God make everything through God's own, interior Word,

14

the Logos, Jesus Christ. In the artist's experience, this rational concept, this word issues from the soul as from a father. Through the process of thinking and then speaking, the soul generates its own word.

The sacramental ministry of the Church depends upon on this same sort of ongoing generation. St. Thomas observes how the Word of God demonstrates to us that God has "insight" which he longs to impart to us. The preacher engages in an act of re-creation by expounding God's Word within the liturgy that re-presents God's saving actions. As an efficacious expression of God's eternal Word, the preacher participates in the creative power of God the Father by giving life to those who listen and assent. In the liturgy, the Church continues to rely on the preacher to make plain and accessible the "insight" of God so as to enlighten and actualize the celebrated Paschal Mystery in the lives of believers.

The Holy Spirit makes present the wonders of God in the Word of God whenever it is proclaimed liturgically. The liturgical homily aims not at understanding only; rather, the homiletic expression of divine insight makes palpable the riches of the heart of the Father so as to inculcate divine indwelling with God's children. That invitation to ultimate communion is perfected in the Eucharist.

Preaching and Actualization of the Liturgy

We know that the liturgy of the Word and the liturgy of the Eucharist together form one single, undivided act of worship. In the liturgy, Christ continues the ongoing work of redemption through the agency of the Church. Every liturgy makes present and actualizes the saving deeds of the Paschal Mystery celebrated. Transcending the constraints of time, the event of Christ's dying and rising unceasingly abides and draws everything toward new life.

As a result, because of its convoking and vivifying power, the term "liturgy" refers not simply to the celebration of divine worship but also to the proclamation of the Gospel. For liturgical preaching remains an indispensable instrument of redemption that actualizes the Paschal Mystery so as to quicken and galvanize the faith-life of believers through the re-presentation of the Gospel.

It is as High Priest that Christ continues the work of redemption, and in the liturgy the Church shares in and images Christ's priesthood.

For the prophetic dimension of the priesthood of Christ appears in his proclamation of Good News. The faithful, therefore, do not experience some contrived or derivative version of God's Word in the liturgy, but rather the mediation of the very voice of Christ himself. This voice continues to resound in the exhortation of the preacher who engages God's people, animating and energizing them with the salvation offered through the Word of God.

Every liturgical action exists as an encounter between Jesus Christ and the Church. Because of the saving dynamics of the Word of God, that divine encounter assumes the most intimate and personal dimension. In fact, the Word of Christ liturgically actualizes the love of the Father in the Church by drawing the faithful into a transforming, mystical *conversation*: "A sacramental celebration is a meeting of God's children with their Father, in Christ and the Holy Spirit; this meeting takes the form of a dialogue, through actions and words" (CCC 1153). The preacher is commissioned to carry on that dialogue through the inspired discourse of the liturgical homily.

The preached Word of God provides a response of faith to symbolic, liturgical actions that discloses their transcendent meaning. Preaching accompanies liturgical word and action to enliven them so that the faithful may readily appropriate the divine initiative offered therein. The mystagogical aspect of liturgy aims to initiate people into the mystery of Christ by proceeding from the visible, sign-aspect of the sacraments, to the invisible yet real mysteries signified. Preaching uniquely effects this process of more perfect integration into Christ via the word-signs of the homily that direct the minds and hearts of the faithful to grasp and assimilate mysterious, life-changing meaning.

PREACHING AND THE EFFECTS OF THE LITURGY

As the preacher's word expresses the meaning of the liturgical celebration, it simultaneously enables the believer to meditate beneficially on the Word of God so that the mystery gets imprinted in the heart's memory and then is expressed in the believer's life.

The twofold dynamic that constitutes the goal of liturgy — contemplation leading to evangelical action — relies centrally upon the agency of the preached word. For one of the principal tasks of the preacher is to provide the congregation of the faithful with words to express their faith, and with words to express the human realities to which this faith responds. Under the inspiration of the Holy Spirit, the saving Word of God nourishes and develops the faith in the hearts of believers into a living relationship with Christ so that they can live out the meaning of what they hear and do in the celebration, and bear witness to it in the world. The hallmark of our living relationship with the Word is our own desire to generate the Word.

PART ONE:
REFLECTIONS ON THE
SUNDAY GOSPELS

First Sunday of Advent

Awaiting Grace With Grace
Mark 13:33-37

As we await the coming of Christ at Christmas on the first Sunday of Advent, Jesus recounts a story about a man leaving home to travel abroad. In our preparation for the birth of Jesus, we do "know when the [appointed] time will come" — namely, December 25. And yet, our knowledge of the historical occurrence of the Incarnation in no way dispenses us from the kind of watchfulness and vigilance Jesus insists on today.

Jesus refers to sleeping in order to symbolize the evil of being ill-prepared and inattentive to the master's return. In other words, the great Advent virtue is wakefulness; we are to be fully conscious in every respect. And our attentiveness must first be directed to the very instructions the Lord gives us today. For in them, if we are alert, we will find a clue to how our attentiveness prepares us to receive the Master so as to participate fully in his life, death, and Resurrection.

It helps to note that today's reading appears in Mark's Gospel just immediately before chapter fourteen, which begins the Passion narrative. That is to say, the passage provided by the liturgy to prepare us for the birth of Jesus was originally written by the evangelist to prepare us for the death of Jesus. And yet, the two objectives are not opposed. For the Church reminds us that everything that Jesus did, from the beginning until the day when he was taken up to heaven, is to be seen in the light of the mysteries of Christmas and Easter. These two great mysteries taken together complete and perfect our personal participation in the saving actions of Jesus Christ.

Therefore, as we prepare for the Lord's coming, our preparation does not cease once he arrives. Rather, the presence of Jesus Christ in our midst only further emboldens us to be one with him in his Passion. That is why Jesus gives us a special reminder about the possible times that the Master might appear. He may come at dusk, as he does at the Last Supper. He may come at midnight, as he does in the garden of Gethsemane when he is handed over by his betrayer. He may come when the cock crows — the time that Peter denies him. Or he may come at early dawn: the time of the Resurrection.

Therefore, unlike the disciples sleeping in Gethsemane while Jesus experiences his agony, we remain wide awake with the Lord this Advent, attentive to his presence, praying in his company, willing even to suffer with him. We vigilantly stay on guard against all personal laxity, laziness, sinfulness, and apathy. And we know that we will be successful in our efforts to be watchful and awake. For the Master has left us his servants "in charge." He has blessed us with the grace, the desire, and the ability to seek him, to wait for him, to find him, and to respond to him in a way that exceeds our natural capacities. And that supernatural capacity to welcome and to embrace the Master in the way that he deserves is the great grace and privilege of this holy season of Advent.

SECOND SUNDAY OF ADVENT

THE HUMILITY OF THE GOOD NEWS
Mark 1:1-18

The evangelist Mark today declares that here "is the beginning of the gospel of Jesus Christ." This announcement signals, not just the beginning of the Gospel book, but more importantly our entrance into the Good News which is the life and saving ministry of Jesus Christ. Advent is the time for us to take up that Good News again and to reconsider how central a role the truth of the Gospel plays in forming the actions of our daily life.

The keynote of our initiation into the Gospel is humility. The "straight path" we prepare to make ready "the way of the Lord" clears away all the self-centeredness, pride, ego, and ambition that clutter up our life and obstruct our relishing the Good News.

In this effort, John the Baptist remains our model. The Gospel's deliberate detailing of the Baptist's off-putting diet and dress confronts us with a curious paradox. Despite John's eccentric manner, we are told that all the Judean countryside and the people of Jerusalem went out to him in great numbers. Something extraordinarily compelling drew the crowds out into the desert, despite John's peculiar ways. They must have been attracted by the integrity and conviction of his holiness, which radiated more effectively than his appearance detracted.

John's self-deprecating demeanor accentuates the poignancy of his message. To receive the Lord demands a radical self-knowledge and self-emptying that begin with the renunciation of personal sin in repentance. It requires a humility that reminds us of our unworthiness and our need to grow in perfection. It calls for a docility that draws us out of the busy distractions of our life and into the desert where we are purified and given a new beginning.

But Advent humility doesn't end with the confession of sins. What a temptation it must have been for John the Baptist to be enveloped by so many devoted throngs who made him the center of their attention. And yet, John's word and example remind us that Jesus is the sole focus of our

Advent preparations. Just as the Baptist would not permit the people to fixate on him, neither should we be preoccupied with ourselves.

Rather, the humility which we receive as a principal grace of Advent reassures us of the three Gospel truths that John proclaims to the people. Jesus is the most powerful one. We are to settle for nothing less. For the power of Jesus overwhelms and transforms all the false forces in our life in which we might try to find our strength and value. Jesus alone is the all-worthy one.

And yet, even though we are not fit to untie his sandals, the Lord will wash his disciples' feet before laying down his life for them. Christ imparts his worthiness to us if we are humble enough to accept it. And Jesus baptizes us in the Holy Spirit. The New Life that comes to us at Christmas in the birth of a Child is only the beginning of the Good News. Its culmination comes when the gift of the Spirit draws us up to share in God's own life.

Third Sunday of Advent

Living in the Truth
John 1:6-8, 19-28

The Church again and again teaches that Christ reveals man to himself and brings to light the human person's exalted vocation. In today's Gospel, the priests and Levites sent from the officials in Jerusalem need to know John the Baptist's real identity. They ask: "Who are you? What do you have to say for yourself?" They have witnessed John's extraordinary ability to draw people out of the city, enabling them to come to terms with their own sins.

The delegates are convinced that anyone who can get the people to recognize the truth about themselves must himself have special access to the truth. They insist that John must be the Messiah, or Elijah, or at the very least a prophet. They demand a credible explanation of why he accomplishes such exalted feats. They seem threatened by his power.

John draws others to the truth because he himself lives deeply in the truth. That truth is the source of his joy and of his unflappable peace in the midst of their insistent interrogation. John states the truth about himself in three clear statements that help us who are seeking to live more deeply in the truth this Advent. He explains his vocation by turning directly to Jesus Christ.

First, John declares absolutely: "I am not the Messiah." The one sent by God as a witness to testify to the light has no delusions of grandeur. Even though "all might believe through him," John does not mistake his ability with the true light, who is Jesus. He does not allow his power and status to deceive him about the source of his true identity. Like John, the more we remind ourselves who we are not, the more do we prepare the way to discover our true identity and vocation in Christ. We permit Christ to be our Messiah.

Second, John asserts that he is not worthy to unfasten the sandal strap of Jesus. He possesses no inherent right or privilege to associate himself with the Messiah. But in humbly accepting his own unworthiness, John disposes himself to receive the richness of God's mercy and to understand the fullness of human dignity that Christ manifests to us. Humility is truth. And the humility that begins in prostrated reverence before the feet of Jesus leads us to the glory of eating and drinking his Body and Blood. In that act we discover the true meaning of our life as we rejoice in the God-given privilege to be Christ's Body. Jesus, who alone makes us worthy of such an honor, himself reveals our exalted vocation.

John's final statement evokes an air of mystery: "There is one among you whom you do not recognize." The delegates assume John is a man of God because of his remarkable words. But John informs them that their old prejudices and preconceptions are not enough. To recognize the Messiah requires a willingness to look beyond bold words and miraculous actions. Rather, we recognize the Messiah as we submit the entirety of our lives to him to be saved. We discover the truth about the Messiah only as we live that truth in our own lives. And the Truth who is Jesus Christ fills us with the grace to face the truth about ourselves with confidence.

FOURTH SUNDAY OF ADVENT

THE BLESSING OF THE BLESSED VIRGIN MARY
Luke 1:26-38

On this last Sunday before Christmas, the Church focuses our attention on how it all began. One might wonder why this Gospel of the Annunciation wasn't proclaimed on the first Sunday of Advent as a start to the season. And, since we already heard this same Gospel read on the solemnity of the Immaculate Conception just a few weeks ago, why bother to repeat it again today?

The reason is very important. God wants us to enter into the mystery of the Incarnation being deeply united to the Blessed Mother. We have waited longingly all Advent for the coming of Jesus. The Blessed Mother is given to us now to deepen our understanding and appreciation of the gift of her Son. United in Mary, at Christmas we can love the infant Jesus, not just with our own love, but with the very love of the Mother of God.

This Gospel reveals the tender devotion that God shows to Mary, and it summons us to join him in giving Mary that same devotion. At the same time, the Gospel invites us into the saving encounter between Mary and the archangel so that we might share in the powerful graces imparted in that exchange.

Upon arriving in Nazareth, the first thing Gabriel does is to declare God's happiness with Mary: "Hail, full of grace, the Lord is with you!" Before announcing her vocation, the angel wants Mary to be convinced of how much delight God takes in her. And he wants Mary actively to share in that delight: "Rejoice!" For knowledge of the profound delight and favor God takes in us fills us with the faith and fortitude we need to carry out his will. Our union with the Blessed Mother assures us how much God is pleased with us. That assurance bolsters us to embrace the graces of Christmas.

Our closeness to the Blessed Mother also acts to free us from fear. Mary could accept the miracle of conceiving the "Son of the Most High" because of the wonder of divine power she experienced at that moment:

when the angel commanded her, "Do not be afraid, Mary," Mary was fearful no longer. The same God who can liberate us from the most enslaving fears is the God who is capable of effecting the greatest wonders in our life. If we let him. God gives us Mary at Christmas so that we can confide our fears to him through her. In response, the Lord blesses us with the same confidence and strength that transforms Mary. God gives us the name of Jesus.

And God gives us the Blessed Mother at Christmas to help us believe in all the impossibility that the Incarnation overcomes. God does not want us to confront the apparent bleakness and hopelessness of our life alone. Christmas is a time of new beginning, of God breaking through the darkness to come into our lives and proving that "nothing [is] impossible for God." The Lord blesses us with his Mother that we might espouse her own trust in this great truth.

Holy Family Sunday

The Holy Family, the Holy Trinity, and Holy Unity
Luke 2:22-40

Jesus' first experience of humanity does not happen in solitude or isolation — like Adam in the garden of Eden. Rather, the New Adam's Incarnate encounter with the world occurs within the embrace of his particular human family. The Church honors the Holy Family today to emphasize the function of the family in our own human development and growth, to stress the role of the Holy Family in deepening our relationship with God, and to remind us how the Holy Family serves as an enduring icon of that external exchange of love which is the Blessed Trinity. In effect, the Holy Family is a kind of recreated Garden of Eden. The original unity of the family stands as the standard for all unity in life.

The Gospel shows us the Holy Family doing three things that manifest their holiness and that invite us to emulate them. We first meet them worshiping in the temple. The life of the Holy Family is formed by devout faith marked by prayer and sacrifice. Their communal act of consecration reveals how we come to discover our true human dignity and worth in the sacrifices our family makes in faith. The piety a child demonstrates towards his parents becomes the foundation for a lifetime reverence toward God. In the same way, children who witness their parents worshiping God become blessed with the ability to understand and believe in the truth of God's love for them. For children identify the way God loves them with that first love they experience from their parents.

Second, we also see the Holy Family together accepting suffering in their life. For Simeon, the Holy Family is the fulfillment of a long-held hope. When he takes the child Jesus in his arms he also happily accepts the reality of his own death, blessed with the assurance that the "light and glory" of God has appeared in Jesus. But the hope the Holy Family gives to Simeon has a price: Jesus will be opposed and Mary too "a sword will pierce." "The thoughts of many hearts may be revealed" only through the suffering of the Holy Family. But the trust, commitment, selflessness, and confidence they share fill them with the assurance and strength they need to fulfill God's will with courage. The peace of the family provides the profound understanding we need to see how God uses suffering to fulfill his divine Providence. The security of the family equips us to confront and overcome the insecurity of life.

Third, however, the Holy Family's love is not inward and exclusive. It reaches out to the world, beginning with the prophetess Anna who "gave thanks to God and spoke about the child to all. . . ." Just as the love of the Holy Family transformed all "who were awaiting the redemption of Jerusalem," so too does the charity and outreach of every family rooted in Christ upbuild and perfect human society. The goodness experienced within the family achieves its perfection as it is zealously and generously directed toward the common good of all.

The model of the Holy Family assures us that every Christian family is that community and place of grace where we too grow in size, strength, and wisdom. As we enter into the faith, hope, and love of the Holy Family, we come to share more deeply in the very holiness of the Blessed Trinity.

Mary, the Mother of God

The Maternity of Mary in Our Life of Faith
Luke 2:16-21

The first hint that the Mother of God plays a crucial role in the shepherds' coming to Christ is the fact that they "went with haste" to Bethlehem. We have already heard this expression in the Gospel. Mary goes in haste to the city of Judah (Lk 1:39) for the Visitation. The hastening of the shepherds to Jesus imitates the hastening of Mary to Elizabeth. In other words, the shepherds follow the model of Mary. They carry on in the pattern set by the Mother of God. The shepherds' hastening to Bethlehem is not simply a courtesy call. Like the Visitation, it is a sacred encounter with grace that transforms them. And the Mother of God is instrumental in that transformation.

Three key things happen through Mary once the shepherds arrive in Bethlehem. We are told that they "found Mary and Joseph, and the babe lying in the manger." The Mother of God remains essential to our ability to find her Son because Mary is the one who first found favor with God (Lk 1:30). Jesus promises that the one who searches finds (Lk 11:10). One proof of his words is the fact that Mary finds her lost Son when she searches for him in the temple (Lk 2:46).

Remarkably, the three chief parables about losing and finding involve shepherds, a woman, and the relationship between parents and children (Lk 15:4-5). This suggests that the encounter of the shepherds with the Mother of God and her newborn Son provides the foundation for our understanding and our embrace of the Kingdom of God.

Moreover, we are told that once the shepherds saw, they understood that "which had been told them concerning this child." In a mystical way, the presence of the Mother of God enables the shepherds to see beyond this very down-to-earth scene and to grasp its heavenly, supernatural significance. The Blessed Virgin Mary acts to mediate the saving meaning of this revelation.

This dynamic is found throughout the Gospel. The apostles saw Christ's glory in the Transfiguration (Lk 9:32). In addition, when the centurion saw the crucifixion, he exclaimed: "Certainly, this man was innocent!" (Lk 23:47). In the Transfiguration, the apostles hear the Father's voice. At the Passion, the centurion makes his confession after Jesus commends himself to the Father. This first meeting of Jesus in Bethlehem prepares all disciples to recognize him as the Son of God. The Mother of God enables us to see the Father at work in her Son and in our own lives as well.

And finally, "the shepherds returned, glorifying and praising God for all they had heard and seen." Since the Word of God could not yet speak, whatever they heard must have come from the lips of God's Mother. And what they saw they beheld in the arms of the Mother of God. The men return to their lives, no longer as shepherds, but as astonishing evangelizers — as good shepherds. Mary is the Mother of the Good News that they proclaim.

Mary "kept all these things, pondering them in her heart" so that future generations might experience the transforming power of her motherhood and benefit from the graces of coming to know Jesus through her. Mary continues to give us the Name of her Son to be our salvation and our joy.

SECOND SUNDAY AFTER CHRISTMAS

ACCEPTING THE GIFT OF CHRISTMAS
John 1:1-18

The Gospel of the Sunday after Christmas greets us with a sobering thought about Jesus and ourselves: "The world did not know him . . . his own people did not accept him." These opening words of the Gospel of John remind us forcefully that it is not enough that Jesus comes to us; we must go to Christ and give ourselves to him at Christmas. For it is only in the full gift of ourselves that we come to understand and possess the gift of the Incarnation.

The Gospel promises three benefits to those who accept the Word of God. Christ empowers those who accept him to become children of God. They are empowered, blessed, and loved. Why, after enduring long years of childhood and adolescence, would we want to give up the maturity of adulthood to become a child? Because the spiritual childhood offered to us through the nativity of Jesus prepares us for the joys of heaven. Jesus will teach us when he becomes an adult that only those who change and become like little children will enter the Kingdom of God.

Therefore, the childhood that the Lord bestows on those who accept him is not weakness but rather, as Jesus himself informs us, power. True children of God are blessed with the power not to rely on themselves. They look to God for their sense of self-worth, their purpose, their vocation, their dignity. As we accept Jesus, the Lord instills in us new innocence and purity. To accept the grace of childhood means to be able to know and love God as Father. To accept the Son of God entitles us to receive the inheritance due true children of God. To accept Jesus in this way is to welcome the life of hope that he reveals.

Those who accept Jesus and welcome the dwelling of the Word become flesh among us are blessed to see his glory. For in the Incarnation the invisible God becomes visible. "No one has ever seen God. God the only Son has revealed him." What is this glory that we begin to see as we embrace Christ at Christmas? It is the splendor that the divine nature and human nature now coexist in the Person of Jesus Christ. The divine

Word dwells among us — not just in our neighborhood, but in our very heart and soul. And because we welcome this divine indwelling in the very depths of what makes us human, we will see God's glory in ourselves.

Through the love with which we welcome Jesus, God unites our lowly nature with his sublime, supernatural one. Part of the glory that we see because of Christ is a new way of seeing ourselves. The more we let Jesus in, the more do we realize how much Christ transforms our weaknesses and imperfections. In Jesus we see that God's glory is for his people to be fully alive with the divine life that he makes visible at Christmas. To recognize and participate in this glory requires our constant, unwavering faith.

And those who accept Jesus have a share of his fullness, "love following upon love." The love of Christ that we begin to experience at Christmas will never end and has no limit. Christmas love will lead us to every dimension of the love of Jesus as it is manifested in his teaching, his healings, his miracles, and finally the laying down of his own life out of love for us. Love will follow upon love in our lives when we follow Love Incarnate in the friendship Christmas makes possible.

Epiphany Sunday

The Manifestation of Christ in Ourselves
Matthew 2:1-12

The mystery of the Epiphany — which means "manifestation" — begins by manifesting something about ourselves. Like the "astrologers" in today's Gospel, it is not enough for us merely to know that Jesus is alive and living in the world as a human being. That information alone does not satisfy us. The Epiphany manifests our deepest, God-given desire to enter into the presence of Jesus and to be in his midst. Our passive knowledge of the Incarnation comes to perfection in our active, personal experience of that miracle.

The astrologers manifest the sanctified way to respond to the gift of Christmas. It begins by putting Jesus first and making union with him their chief priority. If the astrologers had been totally self-absorbed, and preoccupied with their own affairs and ambitions, they never would have observed "his star at its rising." Instead, their alertness and sensitivity moves them to leave behind their lives for a while, and follow the star. It is as if the astrologers already realize how empty of meaning their old life becomes until they personally embrace the Incarnate Christ who reveals the very meaning of human existence to men and women.

This experience cannot happen simply in our thoughts, desires, and imaginings. Rather, like the Magi, we must actually see Jesus. What the Lord manifests to us on the Epiphany must become the new focus of our life. And the star provides the light to gain that sight.

However, being in the presence of Jesus elicits something from us. As the infant Jesus is presented to the astrologers by Mary his Mother, they are moved to worship. As they report to King Herod and all Jerusalem, this is their main motivation, purpose, and goal: they "have come to do him homage." Matthew informs us that, at this news, they all "became greatly disturbed" because the homage of the astrologers threatened their own security, authority, and sense of self-importance. Sometimes our own reluctance to pray and to stand humbly before God is tainted with these same fears.

The Magi manifest to us the true glory and joy of humbly adoring God. As so many great sacred artists have depicted, the act of physical prostration puts the Magi on the same level of Jesus in the arms of Mary. Ironically, our own humble worship spiritually puts us there as well. It disposes us to receive the justifying graces and the love of friendship that come to us from Jesus through Mary. As we spiritually offer our own gifts of gold, frankincense, and myrrh, we in turn receive the benefits of Christ's divinity, his priesthood, and his self-sacrifice symbolized by the gifts.

Finally, the sacred encounter with the Holy Family changes the astrologers. They leave the house transformed. Mystically enlightened by God, the wise men go home by another route. That new route is The Way who is Jesus, who in the Epiphany gives our life new direction, meaning, and value. The Epiphany enables us to see in ourselves the beauty and the goodness of God, which we are called to respond to in the fervent love that characterizes the new way of our life.

The Baptism of the Lord

Mark 1:7-11

When the evangelist goes out of his way to give us special details in the lean Gospel of Mark, we do well to pay attention. The shortness of Mark's Gospel can be deceiving. Its brevity might tempt us to think that it is less important or comprehensive than the other Gospels. And yet, the poetic economy Mark employs in narrating the life of Christ calls us to be particularly heedful of its contents.

In five short verses today, Mark tells us so much. Jesus proves the authenticity of John's prophetic preaching by appearing on the scene: "One mightier than I is coming after me." But the question arises: If Jesus is more powerful than John, then why does Jesus lower himself actually to come to the Baptist and be baptized? This action recounted in Mark's Gospel — which does not contain an infancy narrative — is the way Jesus identifies with all human beings in their weakness, humility, and need.

Coming to John to be baptized is the first thing Jesus does in the Gospel of Mark. Although he remains supremely more powerful than John or any other human person, the initial impression Jesus wants us to have of him is that he is one of us. He is like us in the way we depend upon each other. Although himself sinless, Jesus is not afraid to be identified with sinners. He docilely approaches the baptismal pool of the Jordan to show us just how approachable he himself is.

But Jesus does not want merely to assure us about the genuineness of his humanity. He also honors us by drawing us into the glory of his divinity. Immediately upon his coming up out of the water, "a voice came from the heavens, 'You are my beloved Son; with you I am well pleased.' " What could have remained a private pronouncement to Jesus becomes a public revelation for all those gathered together to confess their sins.

We celebrate the baptism of the Lord to remember how the Father overtly acknowledges Jesus before the world: Jesus is God's "beloved," his "Son," and the bearer of his divine favor. All those who hear this divine voice in a spirit of true repentance can be certain that what God confides from the heavens becomes the source of our confidence on earth. The Father who acclaims Jesus as his beloved and favored child longs for us to share in that same status. If we come to Jesus to undergo the baptism of his Passion, as Jesus comes to John, then the Father's voice of joy and delight will resound in our lives as well.

The baptism of John prepares God's people for the coming of the Messiah, who "will baptize you with the holy Spirit." Christ's baptism in the Jordan, which prefigures his death and Resurrection, awakens our hope to the glory to be revealed in us. The baptism of John disposes us to be receptive of Jesus' presence. But the baptism of Jesus imparts to us the very life of God. If we are not with Jesus at his earthly baptism, we might never believe he has the power to administer the heavenly one.

SECOND SUNDAY IN ORDINARY TIME

LOOKING AND BEHOLDING THE LORD
John 1:35-42

The theme of "looking" dominates today's Gospel, especially in three distinct ways. We see it first in the actions of John the Baptist, whose entire life was dedicated to disposing others to receive Jesus. We witness the depths of his devotion and vigilance today as he watches the passing Christ. John is moved to cry out: "[Look!] the Lamb of God!" John has spent his life watching for the coming of Jesus.

John the Baptist's life is fulfilled once he has directed others to set their sights on the Lord. Even though it means losing the company of two of his own disciples, John rejoices because they instead follow Jesus. To engage in this first type of "looking," we must be willing to look away from past attachments, enticements, and comforts. To look authentically at the Lamb of God requires a spirit of sacrifice that prepares us to share in the ultimate sacrifice the Lamb of God makes for us on the cross where he takes away the sins of the world.

Moreover, as John instructs his disciples to look upon and recognize Jesus, the Lord acts to give their lives new direction and meaning. Once the disciples begin to follow the Lamb, Jesus turns around, notices them, and asks: "What are you looking for?" They in turn ask: "Rabbi, where are you staying?" And Jesus responds: "Come and you will see." Jesus invites all those who regard him with attentiveness, trust, and abandon to look at the intimacy of his life more closely and personally.

This seeing of Jesus' dwelling leads the new disciples to stay with the Lord throughout the day. And as they remained with Jesus in the place "where he was lodged," the disciples came to recognize Jesus as the Messiah. Looking is a form of conversion.

This meeting transforms the disciples, and it propels one of them, Andrew, to rush to tell his brother Simon about their discovery. Andrew personally brings Simon to Jesus. Once in his presence, we are told that

Jesus "looked at him and said, 'You are Simon, the son of John; you will be called Kephas' (which is translated Peter)." Those who have looked away from worldly concerns and have seen Jesus where he lives are in turn "looked at" by the Lord. As with Peter, this gaze of Jesus sets us apart and blesses us with a new identity, a new name, and a new purpose.

As the Lord looks upon us, we see in ourselves our truest value and dignity which are a reflection of Jesus. And as the regard of Jesus claims us for himself, we cannot help but to respond with our own heartfelt devotion. That is why at Mass, before we receive Holy Communion, the priest holds up that Host and proclaims: "This is the Lamb of God who takes away the sins of the world." The more we keep our eyes, our heart, and our soul fixed on the Lamb of God, the greater grows our happiness to be called to his Supper.

THIRD SUNDAY IN ORDINARY TIME

THE PROVIDENCE OF DISCIPLESHIP
Mark 1:14-20

As Jesus takes up his preaching ministry in the Gospel today, we are struck by three things. The Good News that the Lord proclaims in Galilee asserts a specific priority. Jesus announces: "This is the time of fulfillment. The kingdom of God is at hand!" These comforting words of salvation form the foundation for our life of faith. They enable us to respond promptly, easily, and joyfully to the command that then follows: "Repent and believe in the gospel."

This order in the preaching of Jesus remains crucial for the spiritual growth and well-being of every Christian. For, by presenting redemption according to this pattern, Jesus underscores the principal truth in the work of salvation: that God comes to save us as the result of his own initiative. It is the goodness, compassion, and generosity of the Lord that inaugurate the time of fulfillment. Human beings do not "deserve" the reign of God made accessible to them. The Kingdom of God is not something that can be earned or bought. Rather, God invites us to share in his holy reign despite our unworthiness as an effective sign of his infinite mercy.

Therefore, it goes against the Gospel in every way to attempt to reform our lives without first acknowledging and embracing the promise of peace and happiness that Jesus offers us through the announcement of the Kingdom. We can act to change and purify our lives only after we have made the dynamic reality of God's reign the center of our lives. The program of the preaching of Jesus clearly shows us how the first impulse of holiness moves upward to realize the honor, goodness, and tenderness of God. Only then can we come down to confront our own weakness and our need to reform, bolstered by the knowledge of God's care and concern for us.

Second, as the Lord calls his first disciples to be his companions in

41

the ministry of evangelization, we see how Jesus does not want to be alone. In the Gospel of John, we hear Jesus say: "I am not alone, but it is I and the Father who sent me" (Mk 8:16). In calling Simon, Andrew, James, and John, Jesus in effect makes them the living sign of the invisible presence of the Father. United in the Lord, these apostles testify that Jesus is not his own isolated witness. For these men are invested with the very power and authority of the divine Trinity: "I will make you fishers of men." They do what Jesus does.

This privilege of Christian discipleship is meant to be our special consolation in moments of loneliness, rejection, trial, and betrayal. At such trying times, the Lord renews his call to us who strive to follow Jesus in order to reassure and comfort us. Those who come after Jesus are never alone.

And finally, how shocking for Jesus to choose a seemingly most inconvenient, inopportune, intemperate manner to summon his apostles. It is one that involves leaving behind belongings, careers, accomplishments, future projects, and even family. And yet, God's will is at work even in this to persuade us that God's Providence is greater and more fulfilling than any private plans we might devise. We benefit from the wisdom of God's mysterious will only if we follow.

Fourth Sunday in Ordinary Time

Authority, Silence, and Amazement
Mark 1:21-28

Although in this Gospel passage we are told that the people were spellbound by Jesus' teaching, we never actually hear Jesus teach. Nonetheless, we do experience the transforming force of his teaching. It impresses us by way of a demonic interruption. A man with an unclean spirit bursts into the synagogue in the midst of the Lord's lesson. However, what could have been an irrecoverable distraction becomes instead the welcome way that Jesus manifests his point about his teaching "authority."

We must follow Mark's clues to get at the deepest meaning of this exchange. Jesus is teaching in the synagogue in Capernaum. It is in Capernaum that Jesus heals the paralyzed man to prove to the skeptical scribes that he "has authority on earth to forgive sins" (Mk 2:10). Capernaum is also the place where the disciples argue about their own greatness and authority — the place where Jesus teaches them that, to be first, they must be last, acting like servants, and living like children (Mk 9:33ff). In other words, Capernaum is the place where Jesus reveals that his authority surpasses that of the scribes because it casts out uncleanness, it heals and forgives us, and it gives us holy self-knowledge.

In fact, in the entire Gospel passage, Jesus says only one thing: "Be silent, and come out of him!" But how voluminous are these words. In a few chapters, the Lord will say these same words in order to silence the storming sea (Mk 4:39). Later on, when Jesus questions his self-seeking disciples about why they are arguing, Mark tells us that they become quiet like the man with the unclean spirit. Jesus himself becomes quiet before the interrogation of the high priest (Mk 14:61). For the high priest's questions eerily echo those sputtered by the man with the unclean spirit: "What have you to do with us, Jesus of Nazareth? Have you come to destroy us?" In his ministry, Jesus silences all diabolical assaults and prideful boasting. In his death, the silence of Jesus shows us the depths of his mercy as it gives us the way to withstand every enemy of our faith.

We are called to engage in the silence that envelops the newly clean man. For in that silence, faith takes root and the divine authority of Jesus takes over every dimension of our life. We are told that the people began to ask one another: "What does this mean?" We begin to understand in the silence that accompanies Jesus to the cross.

But that silence is only a beginning. "All who looked on were amazed." Yet, at the Resurrection, the angel says to the women at the tomb: "Do not be amazed. . . . go, tell his disciples" (Mk 16:5-7). The crowd is amazed that: "With authority he commands even the unclean spirits, and they obey him." Modern day crowds will experience the same amazement when we obey the command of Jesus of Nazareth by telling all those we meet about the Resurrection with the very authority of Christ. That is how the reputation of Gospel grace continues to spread throughout the world.

Fifth Sunday
in Ordinary Time

The Gospel Portrait of Jesus
Mark 1:29-39

The first chapter of the Gospel of Mark, that we hear from today, aims to give us a penetrating portrait of Jesus. Today's passage emphasizes three important aspects of Jesus' life.

First of all, the reality and depth of Jesus' relationship with his Father is manifested in heartfelt compassion. We are told that, upon leaving the synagogue, Jesus enters the house of Simon and Andrew where Simon's mother-in-law lay ill. "The first thing they did was to tell Jesus about her." Even at this early moment in his ministry, the disciples recognize in Jesus a tenderness, a solicitude, and a power that prompts them to entrust their deepest needs to him. They trust that Jesus will care, and that he will make their need his own priority. The reverence and worship that the disciples witness in Jesus in the temple now get translated and actualized in gracious works of mercy.

But Jesus' power is not reserved to his disciples alone. Rather, his power to heal is a confirmatory sign of his divine authority and of his mission to bring salvation. The whole town gathered outside the door of Jesus with the ill and the possessed as evening drew on. In the darkness of the night, Jesus is the light of their hope. His presence in their midst moves them to believe that sickness and affliction are not the end. If they can get close to Jesus, then they can get away from the despair that otherwise haunts them. And Jesus is eager for them to luxuriate in this hope. That is why he refuses to permit the demons to speak their words which would only frighten, confuse, and mislead the crowd.

But Jesus' life is not one of unending activity. Rather, he rises early in the morning and goes off to a lonely place in the desert to become absorbed in prayer. And even though everyone is looking for him, Jesus gives himself fully to this consecrated time with God. For in prayer we derive the energy, the purity, and the insight to know and love and to

45

devote ourselves to God's will. Jesus never limits himself to those who are looking for him. What he has come to do is to preach and reach out to those whom God is looking for. The Lord's contemplation moves him to action. His prayer moves him on to extend the offer of grace and salvation to neighboring villages — to every human heart.

In Mark's portrait of Jesus we are given a reflection of what we are called to be. Like Jesus, the Christian's life should be marked with an abiding integrity so that what we profess in our faith is made real and active in the daily works and witness of our life. In the same way, the light of hope we radiate as Christians draws others out of the darkness of their misery to take a risk in trusting the goodness and mercy of Jesus. And finally, as for Jesus, prayer must remain the foundation of every Christian's life. Prayer is the principle for our every action, the motivating force for our life, the beacon that fills our life with clarity, purpose, and holy direction.

Sixth Sunday in Ordinary Time

The Leper and the Love of Jesus
Mark 1:40-45

The healing of the leper is one of the first miracles that Jesus performs in the Gospel of Mark. The priority of this act reveals that lepers hold a special place in Jesus' heart. They are the kind of people that Jesus reaches out to with special compassion. The leper is one of the first people upon whom Jesus lavishes his love.

The irony is that the law of the time forbade lepers to get close to healthy people. Lepers were mandated to keep their distance and to live in isolation. That is why the opening words of the Gospel are so shocking: "A leper approached." By making that illegal move, the leper risks receiving a punishment harsher than the daily curse of his disease. Why does he take such a gamble? Because he sees in Jesus a goodness and an authority that surpasses human law: "If you will, you can make me clean."

We are told that the leper kneels down as he addresses Jesus — an act of worship. Elsewhere in the Gospel, the rich man seeking eternal life also kneels before Jesus (Mk 10:17). But he leaves the presence of Jesus sad because he refuses to give up his great possessions. So too, at the Passion the soldiers kneel down before Jesus in mock homage (Mk 15:19). In other words, the leper is the only one who kneels down before Jesus in earnestness and sincerity. He is the only one for whom kneeling is efficacious because it signifies a depth of faith that goes beyond personal expectations and worldly derision. Only the devotion of the one rejected by society accepts Jesus as the eternal King that he is.

As he witnesses the man's trust, Jesus is "moved with pity." Jesus manifests this same pity or mercy when he frees the possessed man (Mk 5:19). This pity moves Jesus to multiply loaves for the vast crowds (Mk 6:34, 8:2). And this is the pity that the blind Bartimaeus begs for and receives because of his faith (Mk 10:46). The pity of Jesus, then, is not mawkish sentiment. Rather, it fires the hope of those whose lives seem hopeless. It feeds those who follow Christ in love. And it perfects the faith of those who approach the Lord in confidence.

The shock of this encounter between Jesus and the leper intensifies when we are told that "[Jesus] stretched out his hand and touched him." In his entire life, had this man ever once been touched with love? Had he ever been embraced before? The leper approaches Jesus, but Jesus' touch manifests how much Jesus wants to get close to the leper, how intimately Jesus wants the man to experience his love for him. Jesus stretches out his hand one other time in the Gospel: to rescue the sinking Peter who attempts to walk on the sea (Mt 14:31). This touch of friendship at the same time enables us to live by faith and to walk in the truth — no matter how impossible or contradictory to the world it may seem.

Jesus tells the man to keep the healing to himself, but the man cannot help but to proclaim the Good News. As a result of this, it was no longer possible "for Jesus to enter a town openly." That is, Jesus is in effect turned into a leper. Yet "people kept coming to him from everywhere." The love of Jesus overturns all our prejudices and fears and enables us to approach the unapproachable with the very love that has healed us.

Seventh Sunday in Ordinary Time

The Faith That Carries Us
Mark 2:1-12

We hear it said that timing is everything. Mark is very explicit in telling us about the timing of the four people who carry the paralyzed man to Jesus for healing. They arrived while "[Jesus] was preaching the word to them." We understand the significance of this when we recall that it was "while [Jesus] was still speaking" that some came to Jairus to inform him that his daughter was dead. To that announcement, the messengers add the injunction: "Why trouble the Teacher any further?" (Mk 5:35ff). But Jesus ignores what they say, and says to Jairus: "Do not fear, only believe." Unlike the messengers who disregard the speaking of Jesus out of hopelessness, the four who carry the paralyzed man to Christ are carried away by his words. Despite the crowds, despite the obstacles keeping them from getting close to Jesus, the four are carried by a faith that inspires a creativity, confidence, and ingenuity which manage to usher the sick man into the healing presence of the Lord.

So too, it was "while Jesus was still speaking" that Judas arrived in Gethsemane with an armed crowd. Judas betrayed Jesus even as the Word of God was speaking the message of mercy. However, today's anonymous four, who unlike Judas have no right to personal access to Jesus, remain confident that their trust in Christ's compassion will not be betrayed.

And Jesus rewards them. "When Jesus saw their faith," he forgave the sins of the paralyzed man. Jesus acts on behalf of the one in need because of the others' invisible faith that intercedes for him. Moreover, Jesus sees into the hardened, cynical hearts of the condemnatory scribes. They silently accuse Jesus of blasphemy. And yet, they are in fact the blasphemers. For, as Jesus will say: "From within, out of the heart of a man, come . . . wickedness . . . deceit . . . envy, [blasphemy]. . ." (Mk 7:20-23). Just as true faith becomes apparent through the action of love, so too is secret evil exposed to all when we cultivate an impure heart.

49

Jesus is not the only one who sees things in this Gospel. Once the paralyzed man is forgiven and healed, he goes outside carrying his mat "in the sight of everyone." The only other time Mark uses this expression is in his description of Christ's dazzling appearance before the disciples in the Transfiguration (Mk 9:2). In other words, the healed man stands before "all" with the very grace of the transfigured Christ. They are "awe-struck" not simply at the physical miracle, but at the glory of God that radiates from one of God's little ones.

Unlike the secretive, conniving scribes who keep things to themselves, the crowd responds to Christ's mercy by giving praise out loud to God. "We have never seen anything like this!" In the mouths of the scribes, these words would signal bitter dissent. But in the mouths of the crowd, they are an exuberant exclamation of faith. And because they glorify God as they see the true meaning of the man's healing, they will also rejoice to "see the Son of man coming in the clouds with great power and glory" (Mk 13:26).

EIGHTH SUNDAY IN ORDINARY TIME

THE EXPECTATIONS OF HOLINESS
Mark 2:18-22

People come to Jesus in today's Gospel with preconceived ideas about what it means to be holy and how to live out faith. To their way of thinking, a certain kind of asceticism and self-denial is imperative to any authentic practice of religion. They take umbrage at the fact that Jesus' disciples do not fast. And they feel compelled to point out the discrepancy in a tone that suggests self-righteous judgment, if not outright accusation.

Such an attitude keeps them — and us — from understanding the essence of faith-living — and from actually living it. They presume that the genuineness of faith is determined by the degree of one's self-abnegation. But the Lord's image of the wedding reveals that they are beginning in the wrong place in their search for authentic religion. Faith is first and foremost about *relationship*. The actions that faith calls for flow out of that relationship.

That is why fasting at a wedding is patently absurd. Guests attend a wedding in order to share in the joy of the groom. To fast at such an occasion would constitute not only a self-absorbed false piety, but also an outright offense toward one's friend, the groom. To fast at a feast signifies a refusal to enter into the love celebrated by the repast. Such fasting remains self-centered, alienating, insensitive, and smug.

What Jesus' image makes clear is how a true appreciation of faith begins in recognizing the privilege of being invited to the wedding. The fact that the Bridegroom Jesus wants us there is the very foundation of our faith. His desire for us to be present as his beloved ones at a feast that celebrates union, intimacy, and friendship remains the unchanging fabric of Christian faith.

Yes, a day like the Ascension will come "when the groom is taken away." Only at that moment is it appropriate to fast. Why? Not because then fasting takes the place of relationship. Rather, such faith-inspired fasting renews the memory of the joy of the feast and deepens our love for the Bridegroom. Absence — especially of food in the stomach — makes the heart grow fonder.

We, therefore, must reconceive our notions of religion with the same common sense we use to get by in the world. Tears in the fabric of our faith cannot be repaired by faddish ideas or trendy opinions. Rather, even our expectations must be redeemed if we are to live in God's love with wholeness. No matter how tattered the cloak of our faith may seem to us, it remains as precious as the cloak of Christ which people eagerly reached out to touch (Mk 5:27, 6:56).

What Jesus calls us to get rid of is the "old wineskins": all the old baggage, the frames of mind, the categories, and the crutches that we rely on to keep things together in our life. For, to those who possess the Gospel understanding of fasting, Jesus promises to give the New Wine of his Blood. It is poured forth for all, but it benefits only those who are disposed to receive it. Our loving relationship with Jesus Christ expressed in his invitation to share in that outpouring is the grace that disposes us.

Ninth Sunday in Ordinary Time

Stretching Out Our Hearts
Mark 2:23-3:6

The voice of judgment rings out at the beginning of today's Gospel. The Pharisees are appalled as the disciples of Jesus pull off heads of grain on the Sabbath. The Pharisees are obsessed with a presupposition about what makes the Sabbath holy. Theirs is a heartless presupposition that reduces God's holy day to so many rules and regulations to be scrupulously observed.

The Pharisees have a way of looking at the world that acknowledges no exceptions, like David giving the holy bread of the priests to his hungry men to eat. They fail to see that "the sabbath was made for man" as a consecrated time for God to reveal his grace and mercy in all its fullness, as he does on the ultimate Sabbath of the Resurrection. But for the merciless, the mercy of the Sabbath is meaningless. The pharisaic heart perverts God's Providence by exploiting God's design for self-centered, self-satisfied purposes.

A truly compassionate heart would seek to admonish the sinner who had fallen prey to sin. But instead, the Pharisees prey upon Jesus, "watch[ing] him, to see whether he would heal him on the sabbath." Mindful of their spiteful scrutiny, Jesus poses a crucial question to the Pharisees: "Is it lawful on the sabbath to do a good or to do harm, to save life or to kill?" It is a direct, fair, forthright question that demands a straightforward reply. But the Pharisees "remained silent," closing their minds to him. This closed-mindedness, or hard-heartedness, makes the Pharisees utterly obstinate, impervious either to pity or reason. That is to say, it dehumanizes them and those with whom they come in contact. And they revel in their lack of humanity.

One other time in the Gospel of Mark Jesus encounters closed-mindedness: when the disciples close their minds to the meaning of the multiplication of the loaves (Mk 6:52, 8:17). However, this exchange with

53

the Pharisees provokes in Jesus the only experience of "anger" that we read about in the Gospel. (The word "anger"is not mentioned explicitly in the passage where Jesus cleanses the temple, Mk 11:15-17.) Their closed-mindedness isn't slowness in understanding; rather, it is a deliberate, vicious refusal to acknowledge the truth. And it angers Jesus because that kind of defiance is the Gospel's greatest enemy. It categorically dismisses Christ's offer of redemption. In saving us, God will not force our freedom or manipulate our will. Rather, what we ourselves have closed to God we must also open to him.

Jesus provides every grace we need to effect such a conversion of heart. Thus, we hear Jesus command to the man with the shriveled hand: "Come here. . . . Stretch out your hand." Christ could have healed the man privately, away from the presence of onlooking eyes. But he makes this act of healing public to show how his own saving presence makes the Sabbath holy. The more we confront our sinfulness with honesty and candor, the more we emerge from the squalid hideouts of our hardened hearts where only inhumanity festers; the more we stretch out our hearts and our souls to the merciful Christ who is so eager to heal us, then the more we lose our pharisaic heart to gain the tenderness of the heart of Jesus.

FIRST SUNDAY OF LENT

OUR LIFE IN THE DESERT
Mark 1:12-15

As we enter into the forty penitential days of the holy season of Lent, we accompany Jesus whom the Spirit sends "out into the wilderness." In that wasteland the Lord stays for forty days "among wild beasts" and is tempted by Satan. What is the purpose of this ascetic retreat at the beginning of Jesus' ministry, and how does it form our own life of faith?

The "wasteland" signifies a place of emptiness, aridity, and isolation. It is a lonely place devoid of all comforts, conveniences, and consolations. In the desert's brutal barrenness, one is forced to confront the full reality of oneself without amusements, amenities, diversion, or distractions. Rather, one must remain keenly recollected, alert, focused, and active simply to survive. In the desert, Jesus wrestles with the limits of his humanity.

The desert experience recreates, purifies, and renews us. "In the beginning, when God created the heavens and the earth, the earth was a formless wasteland" (Gn 1:2). In the beginning of his ministry, Jesus enters the wasteland to prepare for his work of recreation. For, just as the Lord once found his people "in a wilderness, a wasteland of howling desert" (Dt 32:10), so too will Jesus find human beings in the wasteland of sorrow, suffering, and sin. From his experience in the desert Jesus goes forth to meet us in that wasteland where he shields us, cares for us, and guards us as the apple of his eye.

Similarly, the "wild beasts" signify what is untamed and raging in humanity, especially idolatry, fickleness, and faithlessness. Through Moses, God warned the people who had forgotten him: "Emaciating hunger . . . and the teeth of wild beasts I will send among them" (Dt 32:24). In the desert, Jesus is deeply one with the will of his Father. There he is strengthened for his mission to make God known, loved, worshiped, and adored. The union of Jesus with his Father tames the savagery of our souls. We recall how Eliphaz urged Job to make an appeal to God: "At destruction and want you shall laugh . . . and the wild beasts shall be at peace with

55

you. . . . You shall approach the grave in full vigor" (Jb 5:22-26). This reality is fulfilled in Jesus and in us who embrace the graces of these forty days.

"And the angels ministered to him." Jesus does not confront his temptations alone. Nor do we. God provides us the supernatural assistance we need to see divine Providence at work in every occasion of temptation, to relinquish any attempt to rescue ourselves on our own, and to turn our lives over completely to the care and initiative of the Holy Spirit. We need the experience of the desert to realize how close, attentive, and solicitous God is toward us, especially in moments of misery and strife.

God will not keep us in this wasteland. Our consecrated stay in the desert revivifies our hungering and thirsting for holiness. Our time of prolonged emptiness leads us recharged into the time of unending fulfillment. We who experience the reign of God radically in our bodies and our souls rejoice to proclaim God's Good News.

SECOND SUNDAY OF LENT

A GLIMPSE OF GLORY
Mark 9:2-10

For many of us, Lent might feel like that "high mountain" up which Jesus is leading his three closest apostles today. The season may seem arduous, beyond us, and never-ending. And the Church is sensitive to our struggle. That is why the mystery of the Transfiguration is given to us during the second Sunday of Lent to be the center and focus of our worship.

In order to understand the significance of this event for our own Lenten journey, we might consider the three responses to the Transfiguration that we witness in the Gospel. First, there is the response of Jesus who, in leading the disciples up the mountain, is directing his followers to a higher spiritual level. By leading his disciples away from the world and up the challenging summit, Jesus elevates and perfects their relationship with God.

This initiative on the part of the Lord underscores the need for every Christian disciple to spend time in retreat with Jesus, trusting his directions, and accepting the sacrifices required to fulfill them. Without it, we diminish the possibility for our own personal transfiguration as we remain caught up in the disfiguring forces of the world. To mount this high hill is to ascend to holiness. It is a priceless privilege to accept this great call; only those closest to Jesus — Peter, James, and John — accompany the Lord to this experience of glory.

And how do the apostles respond? Overcome with awe, Peter hardly knows what to say. As they witness the dazzling brilliance of Jesus' white clothes and the mystical conversation of Moses and Elijah with Christ, the stupefied Peter makes two responses that are important for us as well. He declares: "Master, it is well that we are here." Peter perceives in the resplendent vision the invitation to divine goodness that the miracle extends. No merit of his own makes him, or any other disciple, worthy of sharing the confidence of God's greatest prophets and God's own Son. God's goodness draws them there. And their obedience to Jesus persuades

Peter and his companions just how radically God wants to impart his transforming goodness to all those who are one with his Son.

Moreover, Peter makes an upbuilding, reverent, even custodial response. In offering to erect "three booths" on this site, the apostles long to build shrines where this supernatural encounter can be prolonged, protected, and savored. They seek to create a permanent place that reflects the solace and shelter they have experienced. They will accomplish their desire in establishing the Church, but the time for that is after the Resurrection which the Transfiguration foreshadows — or, more accurately, fore-lights.

For the only shadow at the Transfiguration is the cloud of the Almighty that covers them and that communicates God's voice. The Father's response to the Transfiguration is to reveal Jesus as his Son, as the One beloved to God's heart, as one worthy of our complete attention, devotion, and submission. For when we accept Jesus' invitation to elevation, when we delight in God's goodness above all else, and when we embrace the heart and the word of the Father in his Son, then when we look around, throughout Lent and all our lives, we will see "only Jesus."

THIRD SUNDAY OF LENT

PURIFYING OUR WAY TO THE FATHER
John 2:13-25

Very likely most of us associate the cleansing of the temple with the last days of Jesus' ministry after this triumphal entry into Jerusalem (as we read in Matthew, Mark, and Luke). But today's reading from the second chapter of the Gospel of John presents Jesus expelling the merchants and money-changers from the temple at the beginning of his ministry. The recounting of this event early in the life of Jesus signals its central importance in the work of redemption, a work to which we devote ourselves in a special way during the season of Lent.

The evangelist makes a striking editorial comment: "[Jesus] knew all men and needed no one to bear witness of man; for he himself knew what was in man." That awareness drives Jesus, as he cleanses the temple today, to cleanse and purify our hearts of all the error, malice, and deception that keep us from worshiping God the way he deserves.

The outburst of Jesus does not arise simply because God's holy place is being desecrated. Rather, the Lord's "consuming zeal" flares at the trafficking of the dealers because it suggests that a fulfilled relationship with God relies on a business transaction. But holiness — justification — cannot come about by buying a bird or shopping for a sheep. We cannot purchase our way into heaven. And Jesus wants to expel this misconception from the first moments of his ministry.

Therefore, Jesus drives out all the animals and the sellers, along with their sacrilegious notions and approaches to God. In their place, Jesus shows us the right way to relate to the Father — a way that reveals and that calls us to share in his own relationship with the Father.

The sacrifice required has nothing to do with slaughtering oxen. Rather, Jesus himself is the true sacrifice pleasing to the Father. To participate in that sacrifice demands our willingness to be one with the Passion of Jesus through our wholehearted commitment to personal self-donation. The sacrifice that pleases God comes from within the believer, from the human heart that Jesus knew so well, as it is abandoned and dedicated to the will of God. That is something money cannot buy.

The outspokenness and forcefulness that we witness in Jesus today are a powerful display of divine charity. Jesus saves us from ourselves, from our delusions, from our temptations to easy and convenient compromise vis-à-vis God. Jesus will pray repeatedly in the last moments of his life that we, his disciples, might share the same union that he shares with his Father. That union begins today as we allow Jesus to cleanse the temple of our body and mind.

Once Jesus empties the temple of all the impious riffraff, it remains filled with his saving presence. Like so many in Jerusalem, as we remain in the Lord's transforming presence, we will witness the powerful signs of redemption that he performs in our life. And we will come to believe more deeply in the purifying force of the Holy Name of Jesus that leads us out of ourselves and into the embrace of the Resurrection.

Fourth Sunday of Lent

Christmas in Lent
John 3:14-21

Here in the heart of Lent, the Gospel challenges us with three crucial questions: What do we love? What do we believe in? And what do we want?

The evangelist John today prepares us for the Resurrection by reminding us about the Incarnation. We are to look toward Easter by recalling what happened at the mystery of Christmas: "The light has come into the world." But the fact that God intimately entered human history through the birth of Jesus is not enough to turn people away from ingrained patterns of sin. "Men loved darkness rather than light, because their deeds were evil."

The presence of the light of Christ in the Incarnation calls for a response to its power if we are to delight in the New Light of the Resurrection. "Every one who does evil hates the light." Therefore, this moment in Lent bids us to examine our consciences and to evaluate our deeds to see if we live in fear of having our "secret self" exposed to Christ's light.

The Lord understands our struggle with sin. He asks simply that we acknowledge our weakness and our need, and that we entrust ourselves to him just the way we are. For that is what it means to "act in truth." And the one who acts in truth "comes to the light." This is the truth that sets us free from every fear, hatred, and false affection. The light of that grace-inspired action of conversion, repentance, and reform makes clear that our "deeds have been wrought in God."

Once we begin to love the light instead of loving darkness, we become free to believe in the truth of God's merciful motives toward us: "God sent the Son into the world, not to condemn the world, but that the world might be saved through him." When our love remains enshrouded in darkness, then our mind is inclined to doubt and to misconstruing the saving motivation behind the Incarnation.

When we believe in ourselves and in our own abilities in a disordered way, we make it impossible to believe in "the name of the only Son of God." Then there is no need to ascribe condemnation to God, for we have imposed a self-condemnation by which we doom our dignity and destiny by our own self-absorbed efforts.

But by believing in the name of Jesus, we receive a new identity by which we are refashioned and revitalized. And then we avoid the condemnation of looking to ourselves for the meaning and value of our life. We see that the birth of Jesus is God's gift that makes our supernatural birth possible: "For God so loved the world that he gave his only Son, that whoever believes in him should not perish but have eternal life."

Belief in the Holy Name of Jesus compels us to look beyond our earthly life to attain our deepest desire and vocation. United in the name of Jesus, our hearts become purified to know what we really want in life: eternal life. But the gift that the Father gives at Christmas must be given anew in sacrifice at the Passion: "so must the Son of man be lifted up." If we are to share in the gift of eternal life that flows from that sacrifice, then our Lenten song before the cross must be the same we sing before the Christmas crib: "O come let us adore him."

FIFTH SUNDAY OF LENT

SACRIFICE, SERVICE, AND SUBMISSION
John 12:20-33

Some Greeks approached Philip and put this request to him: "Sir, we wish to see Jesus." Philip is a good choice for arranging such an audience because it was Philip who introduced Nathaniel to Jesus. However, it was also Philip to whom Jesus put the challenge, "Where shall we buy bread for these people to eat?" before the miracle of the multiplication of the loaves. Philip failed that test of faith because of his inability to see beyond the meager human resources at hand. And one cannot truly "see" Jesus unless he recognizes and accepts the Lord's infinite authority, power, and majesty.

For this reason, when Philip and Andrew present Jesus with the Greeks' request, the Lord does not respond simply or directly. Rather, Jesus makes a ponderous and perhaps even puzzling reply. The Lord answers by informing them that the hour has come for him to be "glorified." These closing moments before the Passion are not a time for the merely curious. To see Jesus means first of all uniting ourselves to the *sacrifice* that fulfills his human mission.

Only the one who "hates his life in this world will keep it for eternal life." And eternal life is the life that Jesus longs for all people to see in himself. That is why to see Jesus is to accept that the grain of wheat must fall to the earth and die in order to produce much fruit. To see Jesus means seeing and loving the potential for eternal life he offers us by inviting us to participate in his Paschal sacrifice. That means sacrificing worldly loves and desires and making Jesus' priority our own.

Moreover, in order to see Jesus, we must first know how to find him. Jesus instructs us: "Where I am, there shall my servant be also." However, *service* of the Lord does not mean subservience, but rather discipleship: "Let him follow me." To see Jesus requires dedication, devotion, and wholehearted, personal commitment. Because to see Jesus means to see and share in the way he himself selflessly serves the Father. And, as Jesus tells Philip later in the Gospel of John, "He who has seen me has seen the Father" (Jn 14:9). Jesus demands the service of discipleship from those who long to see him so that they might enjoy the true honor of the Father.

To see Jesus also requires a *submission* undeterred by fear, hardship, or pain. It means approaching Jesus with the same confident obedience with which Jesus approached his "hour." To see Jesus means seeing beyond the agony of present afflictions so as to perceive the power and compassion of divine Providence at work in every human misery.

A dispute arises amidst the crowd of bystanders about the Father's voice. Some claim it's thunder; others that it's an angel. How can we expect to see Jesus when we can't hear God even though he speaks expressly for our sake? The point is that we cannot see Jesus truly if we remain mere "bystanders." We are called to share in the glorification of Jesus which is the love that resounds when Jesus is united with the Father in the perfect fulfillment of the Father's will. That is why Jesus draws all people to see himself as he is lifted up on the cross: by our active participation in Christ's sacrifice, service, and submission, the Lord's glory becomes our own.

Passion Sunday

Responding to the Death of Christ
Mark 14:1-15:47

On this Passion Sunday as the world focuses on the death of Jesus Christ, the Church gives us the evangelist Mark's Passion narrative to form our meditation. The central question that this Gospel — and that this day — asks of every believer is: "How do I respond to the death of Jesus Christ? What does it mean for my life?"

The Gospel deftly illustrates the many different responses possible, both positive and negative, along with their ramifications. The negative responses to the death of Jesus begin with the treachery of Judas Iscariot, who keeps "look[ing] for an opportunity to hand [Jesus] over." This "one of the Twelve" not only welcomes Jesus' death — he engineers it. Judas' satisfied anticipation of Jesus' death, along with Peter's heartless denial by the fire, poignantly remind us of the depravity of which we are capable when we do not live in the truth.

A second negative response to the death of Jesus emerges from the lips of the Twelve at the Last Supper table. When Jesus gives them his word that one of them is about to betray him, "they began to be distressed and say to him, one by one, 'Surely it is not I!' " It is a response filled with denial, defensiveness, cowardice, and callousness. No one asks Jesus to explain such a staggering claim. No one dares to repudiate the very possibility of such a betrayal. Instead, the "sorrow" they feel is only for themselves.

A third negative response is the mockery the people make of Jesus as he hangs in crucifixion. Even the men crucified with Jesus kept taunting him — taunting the Word with cruel, hateful words. Surely we're beyond such mockery. Which one of us enjoys voicing the jeering words of the crowd when the Passion is read aloud at Mass? And yet, every moment that we take our eyes off the crucifix, every moment that we make the source and summit of our life something other than the sacrifice of Jesus on the cross, we make a mockery of the Crucified One.

To know the positive way to respond to the death of Jesus we must first look to the woman in Simon the leper's house who breaks her perfume jar and who spares no expense in her ardent desire to prepare Jesus for burial. She suffers the criticism of others, she jeopardizes her reputation, she risks rejection, and she exhausts a resource she can never recover. "She has done what she could." It is essential to be extravagant in uniting ourselves to the death of Jesus. For only in such self-emptying does the "Good News proclaimed throughout the world" make any sense.

But even those who are not prepared for the death of Jesus — if they confront it honestly and openly — can be converted by it. "The centurion who stood guard over him on seeing the manner of his death, declared, 'Truly this man was the Son of God!' " Those courageous enough to look upon the crucifixion truthfully in all its horror and its magnificence become transformed by its power.

The power of the death of Jesus doesn't end at death. Like Joseph of Arimathea, the death of Jesus is a reality that every Christian must be "bold enough" to appropriate and possess. The more we own the death of Jesus and identify personally with it, the more we know the splendor of his New Life.

And, like the two Marys who observed where Jesus had been laid, we must make constant meditation on the death of Jesus Christ the life-giving center of our lives.

Easter Sunday

A New Way of Living
John 20:1-9

Jesus Christ is risen from the dead! And the power of the Resurrection imparts to us New Life — life that is new in every way. The coming of Easter does not signal a return to business as usual, resuming the life to which we had become accustomed before the penitence of Lent. No, the Resurrection animates us with an utterly new way of living. Resurrection is not resuscitation. The New Life we receive in the risen Christ is not a reprise of old thought patterns, bad habits, sinful behaviors, or worldly desires.

Mary Magdalene approached the tomb "On the first day of the week . . . early in the morning, while it was still dark." The triumph of Resurrection is the vanquishment of darkness, of every impulse of sin and evil in the world. The Resurrection dispatches the tyranny of Satan, whose earthly reign enslaves human beings through the absolute exaltation of self. Mary Magdalene goes to the tomb alone but, at the sight of the rolled-away stone, she runs off to find Peter and John. That is, she rushes off to unite herself to the community of the Church. For the New Life that the vision of the empty tomb quickens within her — and within us — is ecclesial.

Why does Mary Magdalene run to experience this event in the company of the apostles? First of all, because Mary Magdalene knows that there she will find the meaning behind the mystery she has encountered. She exclaims: "We don't know where they put him!" That is to say, Mary Magdalene relies on the apostles' leadership in faith to take charge in this dilemma and to get to the bottom of the problem. Mary Magdalene commends herself to these good shepherds to find, not a lost lamb, but the missing body of the Lamb of God.

Moreover, Mary Magdalene's take on the occurrence presumes the worst: "The Lord has been taken from the tomb!" She depends on the teaching authority of the apostles to clarify confusion and to dispel doubts. She will trust the magisterial judgment of the apostles more than what she has seen with her own eyes. When John enters the tomb after Simon Peter (out of deference to Peter's primacy), the evangelist tells us: "He saw and believed." Like Mary Magdalene, we entrust ourselves to the magisterium of the Church to gain the interpretation and illumination that unite us to the saving power behind the mysterious events.

The fact that Mary Magdalene runs to the apostles, and that the apostles run to the empty tomb, emphasizes the missionary essence of the Church. Their running is a sign that they follow the prompting of the Spirit of truth who leads them on the way of salvation. In the same way, all members of the Church to whom this truth has been entrusted must vigorously go out to meet the desire for salvation in all people so as to bring them the truth as well.

Mary Magdalene could have kept the experience of the empty tomb to herself. But the maturity of her faith compelled her to unite herself to the leadership, the magisterium, and the evangelizing of the Church. For it is not as solitary individuals but as covenanted persons that we experience the ultimate power and joy of the Resurrection within the community of the Church. In union with the Church, the early morning of Easter becomes the Eternal Day of Resurrection.

Second Sunday of Easter

The "How To" of Resurrection
John 20:19-31

The appearance of the risen Jesus to the disciples today reveals the praxis for living the new life of the Resurrection.

It begins with getting rid of fear. The darkness of the evening and the locked doors of the place both highlight the degree to which the disciples' lives are enshrouded by fear. But the Lord emerges from the darkness and penetrates the locked room to demonstrate the futility of fear. The same divine force that causes the stone at the tomb to roll away permits the risen Jesus to pass through human obstacles and defenses. The grace of the Resurrection causes human fear itself to cower. To live in the Resurrection means to embrace that saving truth and not to give in to the tyranny of our feelings.

When Jesus appears, he shows them his hands and his side so that the disciples will derive all their power from the Passion. The sacrifice of Jesus on the cross remains the source of identity and strength for every Christian. The wounds of the risen Jesus reveal, not the shame, but the redemptive power of suffering.

Three times Jesus says: "Peace be with you." His words invite his disciples to embrace divine Providence. For the peace of the resurrected Christ is the solace that comes from submitting serenely to God's will at work in our life, no matter how it may unfold from moment to moment. It is a gift of peace that the world cannot give.

The Lord breathes on them the power of the Holy Spirit and sends them forth to be instruments of mercy. Experience of the Resurrection is not a private or exclusive affair. Such personal communion with the risen Lord compels us to share the same mercy that restores and perfects us with others through acts of forgiveness.

The absent Thomas comes to learn of the Lord's Resurrection because the other disciples keep telling the Good News: "We have seen the Lord!" The life of every Christian in word, deed, and example must proclaim the truth of the Gospel. Our ardent evangelization draws others out of their reluctance, cynicism, and disillusionment and into the presence of Jesus.

The risen Lord directs Thomas to probe the marks in his hands and side. In the same way, Jesus calls us to touch his woundedness when we encounter it in our neighbor. The fervor and generosity with which we show divine compassion testify to our own transformation in the Resurrection. The New Life of Christ commits every disciple to be life-giving and healing to those most hurting and in need.

And we are confident that we have put into action all that the Resurrection offers when we live by faith. Like Thomas, every shred of obstinacy and doubt is replaced by the heartfelt confession: "My Lord and my God!" That is what we confess as we behold the Eucharistic Host in elevation. Our vibrant, energetic faith rooted in the Name of Jesus and united in the Church in turn helps the rest of the world to believe and to "have life in his name."

Third Sunday of Easter

From Emotionalism to Evangelization
Luke 24:35-48

The Gospel today presents the disciples disturbed by many mixed emotions at the appearance of the risen Jesus: from suffering panic and fright to being "incredulous" for sheer joy and wonder. Their flustered state serves to emphasize just how incapable human beings are of responding even to the joy of Easter without the grace of Jesus Christ.

But the resurrected Christ generously gives this grace, especially in the gift of peace which subdues our inner turbulence as it restores and perfects all the rich potentialities that a relationship with the Lord promises. The bestowal of peace is a pattern of divine charity that we reenact every time we gather for Mass: "The Lord be with you" . . . "And also with you."

Jesus tempers the disciples' agitation by showing them his wounds, by inviting them to touch him, and by partaking of food in their presence — that is to say, by drawing them once again into the saving actions of the Passion. Because the disciples are thereby truly reunited with the risen Jesus, the Lord then reveals to them the purpose of his visit. Namely, the resurrected Christ stands among his disciples to convince them that there is nothing "ghostly" about Christianity. It is a faith of "flesh and bones" like the risen Jesus himself. And it relies on the dedication of the body and soul of every disciple for its thriving.

That is why Jesus instructs his disciples to recall "my words that I spoke to you while I was still with you." Faith flourishes only through active and applied memorializing. We see the fulfillment of God's promises in the Scriptures in our own lives only to the extent that we open our minds to Jesus and welcome the understanding that the Spirit gives.

At the same time, Christ's disciples are called to preach penance for the remission of sins to all the nations in Jesus' Name. The peace of Easter cannot coexist alongside the tyranny of sin which seeks to sabotage God's peace. The grace of penance puts all disciples in touch with Jesus as it unites them to this saving words and to the healing food of the Eucharist.

Christ commissions his disciples because they "are witnesses of these things." A witness is one who speaks from first-hand knowledge. And we who are drawn into these same transforming graces of Easter also become true witnesses of the Resurrection. Our personal struggles with panic, fright, joy, and wonder are divine invitations to place our confidence anew in the peace of Jesus by energetically bringing that peace to others who are alone in their interior turmoil and who remain in need of hearing the Name of Jesus.

Notice that Jesus appears in the life of the disciples "while they were still speaking" about what happened on the road to Emmaus and how they had come to know Jesus in the breaking of the bread. The more we recall to others the words Jesus has spoken to us, the more all will know that Christ is still with us.

Fourth Sunday of Easter

What Makes the Good Shepherd Good
John 10:11-18

On this Good Shepherd Sunday, we focus attention first on the bad shepherd whom Jesus describes as the "hired man, who is not a shepherd and whose sheep are not his own." For once we know what makes the bad shepherd bad, we can more deeply appreciate what makes the good shepherd so good.

Jesus explains that the vice of the bad shepherd is that he "has no concern for the sheep." John the Evangelist uses the same term for concern or care in describing Judas: Judas said what he said "not because he cared for the poor but because he was a thief" (Jn 12:6). Jesus informs us that the bad shepherd works for pay, and John goes on to remind us how Judas "held the money bag and used to steal the contributions" (Jn 12:6). In other words, the disordered life of the bad shepherd is ruled by worldly standards, venal motives, and duplicitous values.

The heartlessness of the bad shepherd most graphically appears in the cowardly way that he abandons the sheep to the savagery of the wolf. He treats the sheep like a trifle so as to safeguard and advance his own self-interests. And he does so because he does not "own" the sheep; he is not personally invested in or committed to them. In the last analysis, the shepherd's only job is to protect the sheep, and that is precisely what the bad shepherd selfishly refuses to do.

But at this point we must ask: Who is called to be a good shepherd? Certainly every leader of the Church, but that is not all. Every disciple who has been entrusted with the precious gift of faith is called to be a good shepherd of that gift. We are told that, at the cross, the beloved disciple "took her [the Mother of Jesus] into his home" (Jn 19:27). We are called to devote that same care and concern to the heritage of faith that we receive from Jesus because of our union with him in his dying and rising.

As good shepherds, we have to possess the gift of faith so much that we in turn become possessed by it, so that we become self-possessed in the Gospel sense. Moreover, like the good shepherd who lays down his life freely, we are charged to use our freedom in the energetic and committed pursuit of those choices that prosper and propagate authentic faith in the world. For it is in the selfless exercise of faith that we, like Jesus, fulfill the Father's will for us and come to know that "the Father loves me for this."

It seems almost impossible to be such a good shepherd, which is why we need this feast every Easter season to remind us that it is only the goodness of Jesus the Shepherd that makes our shepherding good. We can live out that goodness because Jesus lays down his life for us, because Jesus empowers us to share in the very knowledge that he enjoys with his Father, and because the shepherding of Jesus transforms us in an indissoluble union with himself and with the Church.

Fifth Sunday of Easter

Living in Jesus
John 15:1-8

Four times today, the Lord enjoins us: "Live on in me." But what does it mean to live "in" Jesus? To enlighten our understanding, Jesus describes himself as the true vine, and the Father as the vine grower. In this way, the Lord emphasizes the intimate, organic nature of our union with him. And Jesus stresses our connectedness with him in three ways.

Jesus makes clear that the only true source of virtuous action, of human flourishing, of life itself is union with him. "Apart from me you can do nothing." Nothing. That is to say, any efforts attempted apart from Jesus are good-for-nothing. We cannot self-start happiness and holiness. By identifying himself with a plant, Jesus shows us the kind of humility and openness we are to have toward the dynamic of holy dependency that makes us fruitful.

That same humble spirit distinguishes the depiction of the Father as the vine grower, for vine dressers typically belonged to the poorer classes of people. As the branches of the life-giving vine, we are to submit ourselves to the expert care of the pruner who seeks only our continued growth and ultimate well-being.

Normally, pruning took place twice a year: first at the end of winter, and then again at the end of summer. But in the first pruning, the vines were cut back so severely that they took on the appearance of lifeless, wooden stalks. The spiritual pruning we undergo can seem just as drastic and devastating. But it is equally as necessary. Only as we allow God to cut away from our lives everything that distracts, diverts, and detracts us from him do we become disposed to receive the fullness of the life of Christ.

Jesus assures us that we are clean thanks to the word he has spoken to us. The Word of God cleanses us of fear, of selfishness, of doubt, of false self-reliance, of attachment to sin. Notice that it is not any sharp or violent action that brings about this purification, but rather the tenderness that Jesus speaks to us. The more we open ourselves to the cleansing power of the Word, the more does his new life flow through us. The more the Lord's words stay part of us, the more we will see the answers to our prayers.

And finally, Jesus declares: "By this my Father is glorified, that you bear much fruit." Our discipleship gives glory to the Father because it testifies that the vine grower's efforts have not been in vain. Our fruition signals the obedience, the self-surrender, and the devotion we have offered to the Father. The reality of our abundant fruitfulness is the infallible witness that Jesus is living in us. And that dynamic life glorifies the Father.

What does it mean to live in Jesus? The vine is no a place for us to inhabit. Rather, the vine signifies a relationship that we are to embrace. Being in Jesus is no different from being in love. It is the way we exist. It is why we exist. It is what brings joy to existence.

Sixth Sunday of Easter

Love, Obedience, and Fruitfulness
John 15:9-17

As we continue to bask in the light of the Resurrection, the Church asks us to reflect on the words Jesus spoke to his disciples the night before he died. For, blessed with the grace of the Lord's new life, now we can really understand what Jesus was saying to us. The Resurrection endows us with the insight to recall and to implement the last discourse of Jesus in a way that furthers our transformation in the risen Christ.

Before going to his death, Jesus issues three commands that promise three choice rewards. To fulfill these commands we must first embrace the new identity we receive from Jesus at the Last Supper. "I no longer call you slaves, because a slave does not know what his master is doing." And since Jesus does not think of us as slaves, neither should we regard ourselves that way, no matter how much we may feel enslaved by the urges of our passions, emotions, and longings. Since Jesus reveals to us what the master is about, we authoritatively wield the Lord's ultimate mastery over all human drives. We must accept this truth about ourselves in God's sight before we attempt to apply ourselves to his commands.

"Love one another as I have loved you." Jesus informs us that he has loved us as the Father has loved him. That is to say, the Father has loved Jesus as an equal, and Jesus in turn has loved us with that same equality, with a love that prizes us, exalts us, and puts us first. When we fail to acknowledge or believe in the reality of the way that Jesus loves us, we disable our efforts to love one another successfully.

However, when our authentic belief in Jesus' love for us compels us to share it with others, then we experience the exhilarating joy of Jesus. That is, we revel in the delight that comes from knowing and fulfilling the Father's will wholeheartedly and with utter abandon. Our joy is then complete because we have given ourselves to God and neighbor completely. That is what we are created to do, and the crowning glory of our perfection is the sense of elation that makes our life so satisfying.

Jesus directs us: "Keep my commandments" even as he has kept the

Father's commandments. The keeping of Jesus' commandments makes us friends of Jesus. For these commandments are what Jesus has heard from the Father and made known to us. Jesus fulfills the Father's commandments ultimately by laying down his life for his friends. Therefore, our eligibility for friendship with Jesus requires that we too lay down our life, our will, our selfishness, our plans, and ambitions out of love for our Friend. For the commandments that Jesus gives us are themselves friends that lead us more deeply into the intimacy of Jesus.

And finally, Jesus commands: "Bear fruit that will remain." Since it was Jesus who himself chose us, we will remain fruitful to the degree that we live out of that truth. It is the Lord's choice of us, his initiative in our life, that equips us to go forth and bear fruit. Our productive perseverance in the initiative of Christ assures us in turn that the Father will give all that we ask him in Jesus' name.

SEVENTH SUNDAY OF EASTER

THE PRIVILEGE OF DISCIPLESHIP
John 17:11b-19

Before going to his death, what Jesus has on his mind is his disciples and their well-being. Jesus' prayer to the Father is literally one of providence — of "looking forward" to the blessings and benefits that the Lord provides for those who follow him faithfully. Jesus prays for four chief privileges for his disciples: that they may be one like the union of the Father and the Son, that they may share his joy completely, that the Father will guard them from the evil one, and that the Father will consecrate them by means of truth.

The confidence of Jesus in making this petition flows from the fact that he has guarded the disciples with the Father's own name. Moreover, throughout his tenure on earth, Jesus has kept a careful watch that saves his disciples from getting lost. And Jesus has given them his Word, thereby revealing to them that they do not belong to the world.

This all-encompassing care of Christ predisposes us to receive the union, the joy, the protection, and the consecration that form the prayer of Jesus on our behalf. Jesus prays specifically and concretely for these privileges because he knows too well the ravaging force of human discord and dissension. He understands how easily human beings forfeit eternal joy for venal pleasures. He has firsthand knowledge of the threat and menace of a hateful world. And he anticipates how the world's falsehood frustrates the human craving for holiness.

In this twilight of the Easter season, the liturgy reminds us that the providence of Jesus continues without diminishment in our life even after he ascends into heaven. The question facing us is: Are we open and responsive to the generous care of Christ for us? Do we seek our protection in the name of the Father which is Jesus' gift to us? That is to say, do we find our security in living as children of the Father? Or do we seek our strength and stature in our own name? To that extent, we fracture the possibility for the true oneness of the Trinity.

Are we as watchful of our ways as Jesus is? Or do we scoff at the ease

79

with which we can get lost? Do we cherish the Word of God as truth itself? Or do we prefer the false and seductive words of the world that betray in us an unconverted desire to belong to the world?

Jesus consecrates himself for our sakes. That is, Jesus offers himself in sacrifice in response to the truth of the Father's love for him, a love that asks him to lay down his life for us. The care and protection that Jesus tenders in his human life he perfects in his death. To experience the unity, joy, protection, and consecration of the risen Christ we must submit ourselves to the manner in which Jesus provides for us. By laying down our own lives, we can take up the life of Jesus. And with that life he sends us into the world.

PENTECOST SUNDAY

THE SPIRIT GIVEN FOR FORGIVENESS
John 20:19-23

The account of the giving of the Holy Spirit presented in today's Gospel may provide a sobering counterpoint to the easily romanticized rendition we read in the Acts of the Apostles. For the disciples in John have no clue that they are about to receive the outpouring of the Holy Spirit. Rather, they have hidden themselves away, fortressed themselves behind locked doors in feeble fear and the darkness of evening's dread. They have reached the bleakest, most desperate turn in the Gospel yet.

It is precisely at this moment that the risen Jesus takes the initiative in penetrating the disciples' defenses to come to them. We are told that he "stood in their midst." That action recalls an earlier episode also in Jerusalem, on the last and greatest day of the festival at the temple, when Jesus "stood up and exclaimed: 'Let anyone who thirsts come to me and drink. Whoever believes in me as scripture says: 'Rivers of living water will flow from within him.' He said this in reference to the Spirit that those who came to believe in him were to receive" (Jn 7:37-39).

Today, on this great festival of the great beginning of the Church through the Holy Spirit, the resurrected Christ responds to the terror of the disciples by giving them to drink of the living water of the Spirit that flows from within him. As if to prove the force of his words, Jesus shows them his hands and his side, pierced so that they can literally look within him to see the source of the living river of the Spirit.

The peace that Jesus imparted before his death to keep his disciples from being distressed and fearful (Jn 14:27), and to empower them to deal with the inescapable suffering of the world (Jn 16:33), the risen Lord now bestows anew in fulfillment of his promise: "The holy Spirit . . . he will teach you everything and remind you of all that [I] told you" (Jn 14:26). In the midst of the trauma and turmoil that overtakes them, the truth of the Holy Spirit comes to set them free.

In other words, the most unlikely circumstances provide the occasion for God to bless the disciples with the supreme gift of himself in the

Person of the Spirit. And how astoundingly powerful is that gift: "The disciples rejoiced when they saw the Lord." In an instant, the agony of the disciples flees more quickly than they themselves fled from the agony of Jesus in Gethsemane, and the Spirit's fruit of joy (Gal 5:22) pervades!

Just as God originally created man in the midst of the chaos and disorder of the primordial world by breathing into his nostrils the breath of life (Gn 2:7), so does Jesus re-create human beings by breathing on his disciples. His breath literally "inspires" the disciples with the Holy Spirit in the midst of the chaos and disorder of their fear. This re-creating breath of life endows them with the very power, purpose, and pertinacity of the Resurrection.

And, as Jesus Christ makes clear, the magnificence of life in the Spirit bursts forth specifically in the act of forgiveness. Therein lies the true, divine power that informs the very life of the Church. It is active forgiveness that makes visible in our human intercourse the otherwise invisible majesty of the Person of the Holy Spirit. Nothing but forgiveness can reveal the awesome reality and beauty of the Spirit more exquisitely. And it is as forgivers, confirmed in the Holy Spirit, that Jesus Christ sends us forth.

Holy Trinity Sunday

Baptism and the Life of God
Matthew 28:16-20

These four little verses from Matthew encapsulate the central mystery of Christian faith and life: the mystery of the Most Holy Trinity — of God in himself. This lofty mystery Jesus fittingly confides to his disciples from the height of the mountain in Galilee. In the Gospel of Matthew, the mountain figures significantly in the life of Jesus. It is on a mountain that Jesus undergoes his temptations, that Jesus preaches the Beatitudes, and that Jesus retreats to pray. Similarly, Jesus uses the image of a mountain to teach his disciples not to hide the gift of faith (Mt 5:14) — a gift so powerful that the believer can command mountains to move and to throw themselves into the sea (Mt 17:20, 21:21).

What Jesus tells the Eleven now seems equally as impossible: "Go, therefore, and make disciples of all nations, baptizing them in the name of the Father, and of the Son, and of the Holy Spirit." That place of Jesus' own testing, preaching, and prayer becomes the place of fulfillment where Jesus delivers the pinnacle of Christian revelation: God is One in three Divine Persons.

This episode is meant to remind us of the earlier event of the Transfiguration in which we witness identical actions: the trek up the mountain, the disciples falling down in homage, Jesus coming forward and addressing them (Mt 17:6-7). The hint of the Blessed Trinity revealed in the Father's voice at the Transfiguration is now confirmed in the command Christ gives to evangelize the world.

Notice that they are to baptize in the name — not the names — of the Father, Son, and Holy Spirit. This command signals the undivided oneness of God in his being and power. Each Person of the Blessed Trinity is God whole and entire. As the disciples baptize in God's name, they confer a divine might that saves the believer from false self-exaltation on the one hand, and self-depreciation on the other. At the same time, it preserves us from the tendency toward prejudice, bias, and discrimina-

83

tion as it draws us into the equitable oneness of God himself. The life of the Trinity is the life baptism imparts.

Moreover, Jesus' revelation of the Trinity shows us that God is one but not solitary. The three divine Persons remain really distinct one from another. And as living images of the divine Trinity, God delights in our distinctiveness as persons. Baptism lifts us out of isolating individualism and re-creates us according to the divine Persons. The gift of faith empowers us to become more and more conformed to the divine likeness, which we in turn generously make known to others as the heart of the human vocation: "Teach them to observe all that I have commanded you."

The distinctiveness of the three Persons lies in the relationships that relate them to one another. And just as relationships remain vital to the very life of the Trinity, so are they in our life of faith. It is crucial that we know that Jesus is with us always, until the end of the world. And we encounter that saving, transforming presence as we embrace it in the person of our neighbor. When our relationships with others become a lesser priority, then we do violence to our conception of ourselves and of God. We lie to ourselves about what it means to be alive.

Because of baptism, even now we can begin to enjoy the ultimate communion God calls us to share in the oneness of Trinitarian life, as godly persons, whose holiness is revealed in the sacred relationships we cherish.

CORPUS CHRISTI SUNDAY

TAKING CHRIST AT HIS WORD
Mark 14:12-16, 22-26

Three commands undergird today's mystery of Christ's Body and Blood. We need them, for the simple, almost nonchalant quality of the institution narrative in the Gospel of Mark might tempt us to overlook the supreme significance of Christ's self-offering. These three directives usher us into the graces of this mystery in all its richness.

Jesus commands his two disciples: "Go into the city." It is in the city that Jesus eats the Last Supper with his disciples. Mark's few references to "the city" bear profound Eucharistic significance. As a result of healing a leper, it was not possible for Jesus to enter a city openly (Mk 1:45). But now the Lord quits the deserted places he favors and returns to the city, not to heal a man's body, but to give his disciples his own Body. The vast crowds once hastened out of the cities to be with Jesus in the out-of-the-way place where the Lord fed them miraculously (Mk 6:33). Now Jesus himself hastens to the city to feed his disciples the ultimate miracle of his own Body. Whenever Jesus appeared in cities, the people laid the sick before him so that they might be healed. By commanding us to go into the city, the Lord is disposing us to understand the meaning and power of the Eucharist.

Jesus commands his disciples: "prepare [the place] for us." This place is revealed to the disciples miraculously. Jesus prophecies that they will come upon a man who will lead them to the upper room without a word. In the same way, the owner of the upper room will turn it over to the disciples with silent consent.

However, such mystical cooperation is not enough. The disciples themselves must make ready the place of the Eucharist. For that real place is not an upper room, but the very bodies, the lives of the believers who eat and drink the Body and Blood of Christ. Mark quotes Isaiah who prophecies: "Behold, I send my messenger before thy face who shall prepare thy way . . . 'prepare the way of the Lord. . .' " (Mk 1:2-3). Now the Son of God himself prophecies and commands an even more radical preparation of ourselves. Our heart, our mind, our will, our soul must be spacious, furnished, and all in order in order to receive the Body and Blood of the Teacher.

And finally Jesus commands: "Take; this is my body." Christianity is not a philosophy or a mere matter of the mind. It is the living faith that demands our active response and participation. Just as Jesus must take the five loaves and the two fish (Mk 6:41) before he can multiply them, just as the vineyard owner deputes a servant to take his share of the produce (Mk 12:2), so must Christians regularly, faithfully take and consume the Eucharist if they are to grow in God's grace. It is by eating the Eucharist that we become the Body of Christ.

Tenth Sunday in Ordinary Time

Out of Our Minds and in the Mind of Christ
Mark 3:20-35

As Jesus attempts to feed his disciples who gather together as a community, the assembling crowd interrupts them. But what impedes the disciples even more than the physical presence of the crowd is their adamant dissenting attitude. Jesus' own family thinks he is out of his mind, and the Jerusalem scribes claim that Jesus "is possessed by Beelzebul," whose power they think Jesus exercises to expel demons. The Lord uses this experience of bad faith to teach his disciples the meaning of true faith, especially in three ways.

Jesus first asserts the necessity of unity. Paradoxically, even Satan himself — if his diabolical sabotage is to succeed — must abide by the imperative of unity. For any civil strife, divided loyalty, mutiny, or dissension, even in the dominion Satan, renders every kingdom ineffective.

Authentic faith remains rooted in the confidence that keeps the believer's mind and will united to the truth of God and his Revelation. For such interior unity transforms the believer into "a strong man" whose house cannot be entered or plundered by opposing forces of any sort. His house stands fortified by the truth that sets us free, the truth that knows no restraining. The believer who zealously reproves all dissent and compromised loyalty regarding the Church may perplex a world fixated on the chicanery of the prince of demons. But the Christian's house endures invincibly because his or her dwelling is Jesus himself (see Jn 14:4-7).

Moreover, true faith demands ardent devotion to God who is rich in mercy. The efficacy and splendor of faith appear in the forgiveness that pours forth unceasingly from the unbounded compassion of God. The only thing that inhibits that outpouring is a disbelief in God's infinite willingness to forgive. And yet, the moment that we sin against the Holy Spirit by letting doubt about divine mercy poison our faith, we pervert

87

our conception of God. The loving Father then becomes in our mind a tyrannical ogre rabid to punish sinners.

Authentic faith cries out for a heartfelt acceptance of the truth of God's mercy. Only that saves us from the self-condemnation incurred when we refuse to let God forgive our sins. The faithless "carry the guilt of sin without end" only because they impose that burden upon themselves. Gospel faith rescues us from that curse with the merciful invitation: "Come to me, all you who are weary and find life burdensome, and I will refresh you."

And finally, true faith is essentially relational. There is nothing privatizing, isolating, or alienating about Christian faith. The one whose life is truly formed by faith stands before Jesus as another Mary: "Whoever does the will of God is . . . mother to me." The fervor with which we surrender our own will to God in order to fulfill the divine will, especially in the service of our brothers and sisters, distinguishes us as true people of faith.

Even with all this, the world may continue to think that Christians are out of their minds. But no matter. If we are faithful, then Jesus himself makes it possible for us to get the Eucharistic food that silences skeptical voices as it strengthens the faith of Christ's Body.

Eleventh Sunday in Ordinary Time

The Paradox of Grace
Mark 4:26-34

In the eyes of the world, the Gospel of Jesus Christ seems to be filled with contradiction, mystery, and paradox. And yet, ironically, these very qualities reveal the beauty, intricacy, and force of the Good News. As a result, Jesus does not want to diminish this mystical dimension of the Gospel. Which explains why Jesus spoke in parables.

Jesus wanted to teach followers his message in a way they could understand. That is to say, he used the device of comparative story and creative imagery to prompt people to see how present, active, and involved God is in their everyday experiences. Parables serve as an apt way for disciples to understand the Gospel because they root divine revelation in the familiar. By making the ordinary the principle for his preaching, Jesus guides us to use what is already well-known to us as the standard for coming to know what is revealed only in Christ. In this way, parables help to make the power of Jesus' message even more compelling.

In other words, the parables are a great gift of consolation, for they reassure us that the great riches of heaven are accessible to us through our attention to God's interaction with us on earth. There is nothing foreign, alien, or unnatural about God's Good News for us. The more we ponder how the Word became flesh and dwelt among us, the more do we participate in that divine indwelling.

Today the Lord wants to teach us two particular truths about the reign of God. First of all, it is important for us to realize that transformation by grace transpires within us without our knowing how it happens. In our technological age in which we have such penetrating knowledge of so many things, it is easy to dupe ourselves into believing that we are ultimately in charge of every action, development, and event. That is why Jesus teaches us that the grace of the Kingdom grows in us without the full comprehension and control of our mind.

The Gospel asks us to confine ourselves to the mystery of the Kingdom in order to partake of its abundant harvest. Our attempts to second-guess God's Providence only deprive us of the joy of seeing how the Father himself takes the initiative and engineers the increase of his divine favors in our life of faith.

We are content to let God form and perfect us according to his schedule, design, and plan. At the same time, divine Providence demands that we withhold judgment about our own suitability for greatness. The mustard seed "is the smallest of all the seeds on earth." It would be very easy to overlook it, to dismiss it, to discount and reject it. But if the mustard seed is entrusted to the Sower, "it grows up and becomes the largest of all shrubs."

If we long to experience the flourishing of the Kingdom in our own lives, then we must fend off every temptation to think of ourselves as inadequate, unworthy, and ill-equipped for holiness. It is the goodness of God alone that makes us worthy of God's loving care. The smallness and weakness we perceive in our life are there to get us to entrust ourselves more completely to the greatness and power of God's mercy. And when we do, we become great in his sight, big enough — not to billet birds — but to thrive as a dwelling place of God.

Twelfth Sunday in Ordinary Time

The Farther Shore of Sanctity
Mark 4:35-41

As the darkness of the evening approaches, Jesus invites us: "Let us cross over to the farther shore." What is the farther shore? It is the state of full maturity in our relationship with God, of personal holiness, and of spiritual perfection. What brings it about?

To reach the farther shore of sanctity, we must first take leave of the crowd. That is to say, we must abandon all the popular perceptions, pleasures, and pressures that come from living immersed in the world. The first step toward sanctity is a step away from the crowd and into the boat — one of the most ancient symbols of the Church.

In leaving the crowd, we are told that the disciples "took [Jesus] with them in the boat just as he was." In other words, we cannot attempt to reach the farther shore on our own. That goal is possible only because Jesus is with us. Every thought, every desire, every action of our life must begin by "taking Jesus with us," if our choices are to lead us to the farther shore of happiness. For the farther shore is that promising place that Jesus sees and that Jesus enables us to reach as he engenders our desire for it.

En route to the farther shore we are sure to encounter storms. We need them. For the threat of storms shows us those specific areas in our lives in which we are most prone to fear, in which we are most doubtful, in which we are most self-reliant, in which we are most lacking in trust. Every storm confronts us with a crucial challenge: either we can fixate on the terror of the peril or we can focus on the real presence of Jesus, through it all, sound "asleep on a cushion." For the very slumber of Jesus Christ is mightier than all the savageness of nature.

Sometimes we need to experience our security in jeopardy before we can entrust ourselves wholeheartedly to the protection of the Lord. Which makes the disciples' question particularly intriguing. They don't ask Jesus: "What are you going to do?" Rather, they inquire about the disposition of his mind and heart: "Doesn't it matter to you that we are going to drown?" For once we are convinced about the Lord's desires on our behalf, we gain the confidence we need to reach the farther shore.

In order to reach the farther shore, then, fear and faithlessness must remain as displaced in us as the crowd we left behind. We should not be surprised when we witness the staggering authority and power of God at work, even in the ordinary struggles of our daily life. As we draw near to the farther shore, we should not be incredulous when we see God answering our prayers and attending to our needs, even in intimate detail.

Yes, it is an awesome reality that "the wind and the sea obey" Jesus. But what is even more awesome is the fact that willful, sin-inclined rational creatures obey Jesus, especially when it is so much easier to indulge in the carnal gratification of the world. But that obedience is key to the heart of the happiness that we find on the farther shore. And so Jesus provides for it by constantly offering himself for us to "take away" in the Eucharist.

Thirteenth Sunday in Ordinary Time

Healing and Hands
Mark 5:21-43

The two intermingling stories that make up today's Gospel share something in common: the significance of "hands" in both. Prompted by his daughter's critical illness, Jairus approaches Jesus and asks: "Please come lay your hands on her that she may get well and live." At this request, the Lord changes his plans and goes with Jairus.

On the way, an unnamed woman afflicted with a hemorrhage for twelve years sneaks up behind Jesus and puts her hand to his cloak. Her anonymous grasping at Christ's cloak is the woman's last resort, for she "had suffered greatly at the hands of many doctors and had spent all that she had. Yet she was not helped but only grew worse." The woman had given up on human hands — except for her own, if they could come in contact with Jesus. The evangelist even enables us to read the secret thoughts of her heart: "If I but touch his clothes I shall be cured."

The faith that cures the woman accompanies Jesus to the bedside of Jairus' dead daughter. The Lord puts all of the faithless people out of the room, and then, taking her hand, commands the little girl to get up. Jesus repeats this action with the blind man whom Christ takes by the hand and leads out of the village to cure him (Mk 8:23). Similarly, when Jesus casts the mute and deaf spirit out of a possessed boy, the crowd thinks that he is dead. But Jesus takes him by the hand and helps him to his feet (Mk 9:27). In other words, Jesus goes out of his way to take us by the hand when our spirit is troubled, when our sight is darkened, and when life loses its force. In taking us by the hand, Jesus not only restores our life, he leads us away from the death of doubt.

The question that Jesus asks so insistently when he feels power go forth from him he also poses with equal urgency to us: "Who touched me?" Jesus asks this question, not for his own enlightenment, but rather because it is crucial for us to know and understand. The one who touches

Jesus Christ to his very heart is anyone who reaches out to him in need with confidence and trust. The Lord has no patience for a hands-off attitude: "Why trouble the teacher any longer?"

To use our hands to implore God's mercy or to unite ourselves more deeply to him in our powerlessness is not a bother to the Lord; rather, it is the very reason why he became Incarnate — became a man with human hands.

Jesus tells the girl's parents that "she should be given something to eat." They are to use their hands to strengthen the life Jesus has renewed in the girl. And in Holy Communion we too receive something to eat from the hands of the priest that increases Christ's life within us, and that makes our hands instruments of his mercy for others.

Fourteenth Sunday in Ordinary Time

The Amazement of Faith
Mark 6:1-6

Today's Gospel tells us that Jesus could work no miracle in Nazareth apart from curing a few who were sick. The Nazarenes' lack of faith distresses him. The verb for "being distressed" has the broader meaning of being amazed or taken by surprise. We find it used four other significant times in the Gospel. In the preceding chapter, everyone is amazed as the exorcised Gerasene demoniac proclaims all that Jesus has done for him (Mk 5:20). Similarly, the Pharisees and Herodians are amazed when Jesus catches them in their hypocrisy by teaching: "Repay to Caesar what belongs to Caesar, and to God what belongs to God" (Mk 12:17). Pilate also experiences amazement, first when Jesus makes no reply to the accusations leveled against him, and then again when he learns how quickly Jesus has died on the cross.

In other words, "amazement" occurs in the Gospel of Mark when people encounter faith-filled evangelizing, authoritative teaching, or a self-sacrificing witness to the faith. However, what "amazes" Jesus is just the opposite; the Lord is amazed and distressed at the disbelief he experiences in his very neighbors. And that irony is meant to make us pause and reconsider.

The neighbors of Jesus presumptuously reject what even the enemies of Jesus are willing to concede. What stifles the locals' ability to share in real Gospel amazement is their petty, prejudiced preconceptions. The people of Nazareth do an on-the-spot assessment of Jesus' social status, family background, education, and profession. And based on that reckless reckoning, they judge Jesus to be a fraud: they found him too much for them.

What causes us to find Jesus too much for us? Whenever we attempt to evaluate or refashion Christ according to our own image we diminish and delimit Jesus who has come to reveal man to himself. That

95

kind of bias and dismissiveness restricts our focus and attention to our own deficient experiences and ideas. As long as we adhere to such a know-it-all attitude, we miss out on the splendor and the wisdom that Christ reveals to us in his humanity.

When we believe so blindly in ourselves and in our private world visions, the presence of Jesus in our midst becomes superfluous. We thereby render the Incarnation innocuous. An authentic life of faith, therefore, begins in suspending all self-centered prejudgments, false assurances, and self-ordained standards. It is only in God that God's people find their full self-realization which enables us to make sense of life and all its wonders. Faith blesses us to see how grace and redemption flow out of what the world would consider impossible. That is why God goes out of his way through Jesus to penetrate right to the place where we live so as to transform our disbelieving hearts. The Lord wants us to know and to share in "where [he] gets all this."

We can be assured that, as we respond to our meeting with Christ with openness and receptivity, Jesus will work great miracles in our life, even as he does in this Eucharist.

Fifteenth Sunday in Ordinary Time

True Oneness With Christ
Mark 6:7-13

With only twelve apostles to assist him in his mission of proclaiming the Kingdom of God, why would Jesus send these chosen men out of his presence? The Lord disperses them from his side to preach on their own so that in their commissioning they might discover their true oneness with Christ. When the apostles are physically separated from Jesus they experience profoundly the reality and depth of their union with him. For it is when they are away from the Lord, seemingly on their own, that the apostles witness the powerful effects of the divine authority over unclean spirits with which Jesus endows them. "They drove out many demons, and they anointed with oil many who were sick and cured them."

It is good for the apostles and for us to see the power of God at work in our efforts and initiatives. For that experience of being an instrument of grace convicts us about what it means to live by faith. In fact, it is a participation in the dynamics of the life of the Blessed Trinity. For the Son himself came from God and was descended from heaven. And yet, as St. Thomas teaches, the more perfectly something is emitted interiorly, the more united it is with its source, like knowing which stays with the knower. The Word which the apostles proclaim is the conception of their understanding of Christ. And the more they proclaim this Word, on their own out of the sight of Jesus and with faith-filled conviction, the more intimately do they become identified with Christ.

And just as Christ's whole earthly life is a revelation of the Father, so too is our active discipleship a revelation of the authority of the Son. A revelation first of all to ourselves! Life in Christ truly changes and transforms us. It blesses us with an authority, a conviction, and a self-possession that we cannot concoct on our own.

That is why Jesus insists that the apostles set forth without food, traveling bag, coins, or a change of clothes. These things might distract the devotion of the disciples and tempt them to trust in their own resources and devices instead of in the Providence of God. Rather, they are to be equipped with only those things that enable their continued progress as disciples: namely, sandals and a walking stick. These things insure that they can keep going. And the apostles are to accept the offer of hospitality as a confirmatory sign of God's protection and care.

The message they preach is the need of repentance. For only a grace-filled awareness of our sinfulness and of our need for God's mercy makes us eligible for God's Kingdom. So crucial is this disposition, that those who refuse it are to be given a dramatic demonstration of the price of their obstinacy: the departing apostles are to shake the dust of the place from their feet in testimony against them. An unrepentant heart will not sully the "beautiful feet" of those who preach the Good News (Is 52:7).

The one other "provision" of each apostle is another apostle. For the Gospel of repentance, mercy, and grace is best demonstrated in the life of fraternal charity that the united apostles witness to the world. The empty purses that they carry in their belts testify to the great hope in God's riches that they expect to collect.

Sixteenth Sunday in Ordinary Time

Pity, Piety, and Power
Mark 6:30-34

As the apostles return from their evangelizing mission, they report to Jesus "all they had done and taught." And the Lord confirms just how important it is to reflect prayerfully on our life of faith and how we share it with others. Jesus commands his disciples: "Come away by yourselves to a deserted place and rest a while." This command serves as the basis for the Christian practice of setting time aside regularly to make a spiritual retreat.

Jesus and the apostles "went off in the boat by themselves to a deserted place." The "deserted place" reminds us of "the farther shore" of Mark 4:35. It is a place set apart and away from the crowds where we can be alone with Jesus, to whom we give our full attention. For if we do not devote time to meditate on how God is working in our life, we may overlook key graces and subtle signs of God's presence and favor. We begin to lose the ability to interpret the saving significance of what we do and teach in Jesus' name.

That is why the crucial element of such regular recollection is being in the presence of Jesus. For us, the "deserted place" is prayer before the tabernacle or the Blessed Sacrament in exposition. In the saving presence of Christ in the Eucharist, Jesus supplies for all the real absences we experience in our daily struggles with faith and discipleship.

The people "from all the towns" are so convinced of the power of being in the presence of Jesus that they will not let him get away. They figure out his destination, spread the word to others, hasten to the place on foot, and arrive there even before the Lord's boat. True faith studies the ways of God, proclaims the Good News, and hastens to be with Jesus, anticipating the mercy to be found in the Lord's presence.

Upon disembarking, Jesus saw a vast crowd and "his heart was moved with pity for them, for they were like sheep without a shepherd." The pity of Jesus is never without effect. The Lord's pity for the leper (Mk 1:41) moves Jesus to stretch out his hand and heal him. His pity for the four thousand (Mk 8:2) leads to the miraculous feeding. Jesus' pity toward the possessed boy (Mk 9:22) prompts him to cast out the demon that enslaves him. And in today's Gospel, the Lord's pity aroused by the aimlessness of his followers spurs him on "to teach them many things." In other words, when Jesus pauses to reflect on our suffering, our hunger, our demons, and our wandering, he responds with redemptive action that satisfies our needs as it conforms us more closely to himself.

What the Lord asks of us is that we too take the time to pause in our "coming and going" so as to reflect on our radical need for Christ and on the unique way that he makes it possible for us to eat and to be satisfied regarding every need and hunger in the Eucharist.

SEVENTEENTH SUNDAY IN ORDINARY TIME

SACRIFICE AND THE BREAD OF LIFE
John 6:1-15

For five consecutive Sundays, beginning today, the Church offers us an intensive meditation on the Bread of Life discourse in the Gospel of John. Today's Gospel focuses in a special way on the *sacrificial dimension* of the Bread of Life.

Jesus is concerned about providing food for the five thousand who have been "follow[ing] him because they saw the signs he was performing on the sick." Suffering draws them to Christ in a spirit of utter abandonment and trust. And Jesus reveals that the way he will feed those who follow him in their affliction entails surrendering himself to the reality of human suffering.

The three sayings of Jesus in today's Gospel help direct our understanding of this mystery. The Lord asks: "Where can we buy enough food for them to eat?" The question highlights the human impossibility of the situation while it galvanizes the faith of those who hear. What seems futile and absurd when left to human devices becomes a cause for celebration and rejoicing when faith turns with confidence to the resources of God. To receive the Bread of Life, we must first sacrifice our negativity, our self-reliance, and our negligence towards God.

Jesus tells his disciples: "Have the people recline." That is, the disciples are to form the hope of the people. As the disciples instruct the crowd to recline on the grass, they encourage the people to assume a posture of trustfulness and expectation; they await the serving of a meal which the disciples assure is on the way. By placing their hunger in the Providence of God, the people enter into the sacrificial quality of the miraculous meal that prefigures the Eucharist. Every action done so as to cleave to God in communion of holiness is a true sacrifice. And by taking their places on the ground with their eyes fixed confidently on Jesus, the people unite themselves to the Lord in a communion of holiness.

Jesus commands: "Gather the fragments left over, so that nothing will be wasted." Jesus insists on this re-collection because what the people have experienced is not an ordinary meal, but an encounter with divine love. The encounter that begins on this mountain in the breaking of bread will be consummated on the hill of the cross in the breaking of Jesus' body. This is a love that never ends. And thus the disciples gather up the fragments so that they can be shared with others. Out of the fragments of our lives, God continues to feed us, to heal us, to care for us through the transforming power of grace.

The special care we show the gathered broken pieces reminds us that suffering is present in the world in order to release love. It prepares us to embrace the Passion of Christ which creates good by means of suffering. As our struggles, prayers, and work are united to the sacrifice of Christ, they acquire a new value: the value of Christ's sacrifice to the Father. That is why, to partake of the Bread of Life, we must be willing to make an offering of ourselves that is equal to Christ's. And it begins by believing in the value of every sacrifice made in love, even the small things, like placing into the hands of Jesus our "five barley loaves and two fish." In the hands of Jesus, that offering becomes so much for so many.

Eighteenth Sunday in Ordinary Time

Nourishment and the Bread of Life
John 6:24-35

Today's Gospel meditation on the Bread of Life discourse focuses in a special way on the Bread of Life as *food*. Jesus instructs us: "Do not work for food that perishes but for the food that endures for eternal life, which the Son of Man will give you." At first glance, such a directive may seem illogical and extreme. It we do not labor for the food that keeps us alive, then what will sustain us so that we can work at all? Jesus the Bread of Life provides the answer.

In the Bible, the staple of bread is synonymous with food itself. Bread remains so essential to human subsistence that to lack bread is to lack everything. This identification between bread and our very existence hits home in the most profound way as we hear Jesus declare: "I am the bread of life." To lack Jesus in our life is to lack life itself. Jesus capitalizes on our vital need for food in order to signal our crucial need for Christ. Only by consuming him do we receive the sustenance that not only preserves our life, but that fills it with meaning, insight, and goodness. We become what we eat.

The crowds remind Jesus that their ancestors had manna to eat in the desert, miraculously provided via the mediation of Moses. But Jesus corrects their perception: "My Father gives you the true bread from heaven" (Jn 6:32b). The Bread of Life does not come from a place but from a divine Person. It is the blessing of a relationship with God. If we want to know where the Bread of Life comes from in our own lives, we must be willing personally to enter into that relationship of love. The Bread of Life is not merely a food to be eaten, but a life to be embodied: "For the bread of God is that which comes down from heaven and gives life to the world." Jesus the Bread of Life satisfies our every hunger and keeps us from ever thirsting again.

Therefore, in order to partake of the Bread of Life, we must be willing to receive it with the humility and confidence of children. And that true childlike disposition comes to us as we remain united to Jesus, "the Son of Man," whom the crowd first calls "Rabbi" and then later "Sir," indicating their growth in faith. They ask Jesus to "give us this bread always." In response to just such a request, Jesus teaches us to pray, "Our Father . . . give us this day our daily bread." We are to "come to" and "believe in" Jesus in the same way that he himself approaches the Father: as a child of God.

Therefore, the work of God that we should be about is to "have faith in the One he sent." Our daily bread is the grace to love Jesus as much as he deserves. That dynamic of lived faith nourishes us more than any earthly food because it ushers us into the very intimacy of the life shared by the Father and the Son. Our living faith serves as an imperishable food that satisfies unto life eternal.

Nineteenth Sunday in Ordinary Time

Communication and the Bread of Life
John 6:41-51

Today's Gospel meditation on the Bread of Life discourse focuses in a special way on the Bread of Life as *communication.* The people have listened to the declaration of Jesus that he is the Bread of Life come down from heaven as the gift of the Father. And this leads them to protest: "Is this not Jesus, the son of Joseph? Do we not know his father and mother? Then how can he say 'I have come down from heaven?' " In their skepticism and short-sightedness, they have missed the point.

The crowd does what crowds are famous for: they gossip, judge, criticize, accuse, backbite, and disapprove. This leads Jesus to say: "Stop murmuring among yourselves." Bad talk of every sort is prohibited around the Word of God who is the truth. The Lord's assertion about his identity and origin is much more than just a "claim" — it is a divine revelation that demands a response of wholehearted assent.

The murmuring crowd in effect "eats up" Jesus with their dissent. But anyone who opens his mind and heart to "hear the Father and learn from him" separates himself from the grumbling crowd and comes to Jesus. "No one can come to me unless the Father who sent me draw[s] him." To partake of the Bread of Life is to participate in a new and more perfect understanding of heaven: "Whoever believes has eternal life." In other words, we begin to enter into heaven with its saving effects the moment we look beyond the earthly dimensions of the Bread of Life by giving ourselves to the mystery of the gift with faithful assent.

No wonder we refer to the ritualistic act of receiving the Body of Christ as "communication." The Host in Holy Communion is communicated to us. Jesus asserts: "The bread that I will give is my flesh for the life of the world." And in addition to the other life-giving effects of the Bread of Life, the Eucharist also serves to purify, clarify, and uplift our human communication with others. In the Bread of Life we receive the Word who is the Father's gift. And that Word transforms the words of our conversation and interaction with others.

Just as it is the priest's spoken words at Mass that make Jesus really present in the Eucharist, so does our spoken word, our communication with others, become a force that draws others to recognize Jesus in our midst. The reality of Jesus the Bread of Life calls us to use our human communication for that saving purpose.

Jesus promises: "Whoever eats this bread will live forever." We can be assured of our sharing in that eternal life, for elsewhere the Lord declares: "Heaven and earth will pass away, but my words will not pass away" (Lk 21:33). We who have been drawn to Jesus the Bread of Life by the Father receive that gift in sacred communication. And in that graced exchange we have come to believe in the eternal life conferred in the eternal Word we consume as Bread containing heaven.

Twentieth Sunday in Ordinary Time

Real Presence and the Bread of Life
John 6:51-58

Today's Gospel meditation on the Bread of Life discourse focuses in a special way on the Bread of Life as *real presence*. This Bread is not merely a symbol of the life-giving power of God. Nor is it simply a sign pointing to future eternal life. As Jesus himself insists: "I myself am the living bread come down from heaven. . . . The bread I will give is my flesh for the life of the world."

How are we to understand the dynamism of this real presence? The Lord explains: "Just as the Father who has life sent me and I have life because of the Father, so the man who feeds on me will have life because of me." In other words, the miracle of the Incarnation — the Word becoming flesh — provides the principle whereby we realize the transformation that takes place in us through our reception of the Eucharist. Just as the body of Jesus has human life because of the Father, so are we filled with divine life when we eat the Body of Christ.

"Life" is the key to understanding the Lord's teaching today about the Bread of Life. For life is not the same thing as our body. Rather, life fills the body, animates it, and thereby fulfills it. The Gospel, then, challenges our conception of life. Do we equate life simply with plodding along, persevering in existence, staying alive — avoiding death? Or do we, in Christ, see earthly existence as a prelude and invitation to life with God that never ends — the real presence of ultimate communion in heaven? To convince us of this saving truth, Christ is emphatic in twice repeating: "If anyone eats this bread he shall live forever." Is that the kind of life we want? Because it begins now.

"My flesh is real food and my blood real drink." But the dubious, faithless people quarrel among themselves, protesting: "How can he give us his flesh to eat?" To receive the gift of eternal life now means to receive the gift of the real food of his Body now. Both seem impossible. It is only once we surrender our limited, faulty, self-centered modes of reasoning and of interpreting that the truth, beauty, and goodness of the Bread of Life become transparent to us. The Real Presence of everlasting life in Christ's flesh in turn transforms the very way that we perceive of all "reality." But that transformation happens only as we feed on that flesh. It takes place only as we allow the sacramental life of the Church to take the place of all our skepticism and cynicism.

Jesus promises that the one who feeds on his Flesh and drinks his Blood has eternal life — that is, he possesses that faith which is a true form of knowing God which initiates a real beginning of eternal life. He is filled with the hope and trust that Christ "will raise him up on the last day." And he is assured of the intimate union of Christ's love who pledges to remain in the one who remains in him.

Therefore, even if we are "alive," if we "do not eat the flesh of the Son of Man" we have no life in us. For that Life is given to us through the Eucharist which comes to us only by our union with the life of the Church, the Body of Christ.

Twenty-First Sunday in Ordinary Time

Communion and the Bread of Life
John 6:53, 60-69

Today's final Gospel meditation on the Bread of Life discourse focuses in a special way on the Bread of Life as *communion*. Ironically, this truth is brought into relief at first by the discord and disharmony sparked by the declaration of Jesus: "Unless you eat the flesh of the Son of Man and drink his blood, you do not have life within you." The Gospel informs us that, after hearing the Lord's words, "many of the disciples of Jesus remarked, 'This saying is hard; who can accept it?' " Tragically, "many [of] his disciples returned to their former way of life and no longer accompanied him." They reject the gift of the Bread of Life given specifically to unify and to bestow peace.

Jesus, however "was fully aware that his disciples were murmuring at what he said." Two Sundays ago we heard Jesus silence the grumbling crowd with the command, "Stop murmuring among yourselves." The only other moments of "murmuring" in the Gospel of John come from the enemies of Jesus. In fact, the Pharisees who hear the murmuring about Jesus, respond by sending temple guards to arrest him (Jn 7:32). In other words, such murmuring remains one of the first steps that lead to the death of Jesus. Not only does murmuring sow deadly seeds of dissent, it actually causes indirectly the crucifixion of Christ.

But this time the Lord responds to the murmuring, not with a reprimand, but with a question to his disciples: "Does this shock you?" For "the spirit that gives life" does so precisely by drawing believers together in communion. That is to say, the Spirit enlivens us by drawing us into a relationship with Christ and with each other that inspires us to be united with Jesus in his work of fulfilling the Father's will: "for this reason I have told you that no one can come to me unless it is granted him by my Father." For the person of faith and courage, Jesus' words "are the spirit

109

that gives life" because they save us from the death of isolating doubt and adhere us to the communal life of love shared by the Blessed Trinity.

Hence the supreme poignancy of Jesus' question to the Twelve: "Do you also want to leave?" Simon Peter answers, not for himself but for all the apostles — and for the Church — "Master, to whom shall we go? You have the words of eternal life. We have come to believe and are convinced that you are the Holy One of God." The act of receiving the Bread of Life in Holy Communion perfects our commitment to remain in holy communion with Christ, the Word of eternal life.

In reality, the world was created for the sake of the Church, which is the convocation of men and women in Christ that effects unending communion with God's life. Christ and his Church together make up the "whole Christ" — a wholeness that is revealed in the mystery of the Bread of Life. "Who can accept it?" — how can anyone take it seriously? For anyone who has experienced the blessing of the communion of the Church, the real question is: How can anyone *not* take it seriously?

TWENTY-SECOND SUNDAY IN ORDINARY TIME

THE TRADITION OF TRUE TRADITION
Mark 7:1-8, 14-15, 21-23

Today we are told that the Pharisees and some of the experts in the law who had come from Jerusalem gathered around Jesus. By this action, the Pharisees and legal experts imitate the large crowds who, four times previously in Mark's Gospel, gather around Jesus. The crowds gather in order to hear the teaching of Jesus, to have him expel the demons that possess them, and to secure a cure for the sick. The Pharisees, and lawyers, however, gather to scrutinize and to challenge Jesus.

Their criticism takes the form of a question: "Why do your disciples not follow the tradition of the elders but instead eat a meal with unclean hands?" They assign to tradition — what has been "handed down" to them — a primacy and importance that approach idolatry. This leads the Lord to say: "Their hearts are far from me. In vain do they worship me, teaching as doctrines human precepts. You disregard God's commandment but cling to human tradition."

This hypocrisy, this disordered, self-serving merging of the secular and the sacred is not to be tolerated in that gathering around Jesus Christ by which we are raised up to share in God's own divine life, i.e., the Kingdom of heaven. This gathering is the Church — on earth the seed and beginning of the Kingdom.

And so, in counteracting the self-righteous, isolating, individualistic prejudice of the Pharisees — a prejudice that promotes bodily hygiene over communal unity — Jesus first "summon[s] the crowd again." For only those who gather close to Jesus to absorb his teaching, to witness his supreme power, and to experience his infinite compassion stand predisposed to understand the real meaning of "tradition" in the life of faith. Authentic Tradition, which forms the Church, remains rooted in a faith that embraces the teaching of Jesus as divine truth which unites us to his Person. Moreover, true Tradition fills us with deep reverence for

Christ by which a hope, that remains fixed on heaven, gets set afire. By that hope our hearts draw near to Jesus, clinging to Christ in holy love.

As Jesus makes clear, our true devotion to Authentic Tradition appears in our outward actions: "Nothing that enters one from outside can defile that person; but the things that come out from within are what defile." For our conformity to the tradition inaugurated in Christ transforms "the deep recesses of the heart," rooting out every "wicked design" and configuring our minds, our passions, our appetites, and every human drive and desire to the purity of his divine Person.

Why is that? Because the Tradition that Jesus "hands down" for us to follow is his own human life in sacrifice. He hands it down to us in his Body which is the Church. Our life in the Church realizes in us that interior purity that frees us from sensuality, injustice, anger, dishonesty, selfishness, hatred, blasphemy, and every form of viciousness indicated by Christ. Jesus asks simply that we seek our righteousness in himself, by drawing close to his Person in faith, reverencing the Tradition of faith in hope, and gathering in love close to the Lord in the gathering of the Church where the Lord himself purifies us to receive the food of the Eucharist.

Twenty-Third Sunday in Ordinary Time

Coming to Hear and to Speak the Word
Mark 7:31-37

Today's Gospel provides a powerful lesson about authentic Christian living, the communion of the Church, and what it means to be an instrument of grace. When Jesus returns home to the Sea of Galilee after his long journey from the north, he is met by some people who "brought him a deaf man who had a speech impediment." This demonstrates how it is through the compassion, the trust, and the mediation of others that we are brought into the saving presence of Jesus where we experience his healing and transforming power.

These people "beg" Jesus to lay his hand on the deaf man. No fewer than nine times do we hear of people imploring Jesus in this way so as to gain the assistance of the Lord for the sick, the possessed, and the afflicted. The root of the Greek word for this beseeching is the same that underlies the word "Paraclete" — the Holy Spirit as Helper and Comforter. Therefore, by bringing this needy man to Jesus and interceding for him from the depths of their hearts, the believers of Jesus act in a way that prefigures the revivifying power of the Holy Spirit sent at Pentecost.

The way Jesus responds helps us to understand how the Lord draws us into a deeper and more intimate relationship with himself. First of all, Jesus took him off by himself away from the crowd. It is in our prayerful solitude with Jesus, where we give him our full attention, secluded from all the distractions, diversions, and seductions of "the crowd" that we experience his tender mercy and healing love. For Jesus is never content simply to fix the problem others put before him. His miracles are a way of drawing those in need into a union of friendship with himself. But that intimacy is impossible on our part if we remain caught up in the clamor and the impersonalism of the crowd.

There is a pronounced sacramental dimension to the healing. Jesus puts his fingers in the man's ears, he touches the man's tongue with saliva, he looks to heaven so as to indicate how the Father is the source of his healing power, and he utters a groan and a healing word: "Ephphatha!" In other words, in healing the deaf man, Jesus calls in to play everything that is significant about human existence — especially confidence in our relationship with God — so as to perfect what is defective about humanity in a way that unites us more deeply to his divinity. This saving dynamic continues in the sacramental life of the Church that uses created things, the spoken word, and the responsiveness of the senses to mediate the grace of God.

And Jesus "enjoined them strictly not to tell anyone." But what about the Christian obligation to evangelize? Christ's words reveal that true evangelization must proclaim the whole Christ and the full truth of God's Kingdom. Jesus is not merely a miracle-worker who "makes the deaf hear and (the) mute speak"; he is the Son of God who has come to save us from our sins. Only as we turn our lives over to him in contemplative silence, in the embrace of the Church and the sacraments, and with the holy fervor of a missionary can we understand — and proclaim — that "he has done all things well!"

TWENTY-FOURTH SUNDAY IN ORDINARY TIME

CHRIST REVEALS US TO OURSELVES
Mark 8:27-35

Jesus poses the central question of today's Gospel: "Who do people say that I am?" Why does Jesus ask such a question — one so seemingly obvious we wonder if it is worth asking? The variety of responses given — John the Baptist, Elijah, a prophet — reveals that the answer is not so clear, and that those closest to Jesus really aren't sure who he is. Yet, it is crucial that we answer Jesus' question and that we understand who he is. For the way that we regard Jesus determines the way that we relate to him.

If Jesus is John the Baptist, then we look to him only for instruction regarding moral formation. If he is Elijah, then we might regard Jesus merely as a mystical figure heralding the end of time. And if Jesus is merely a prophet, then he is only a spokesman for God and not God himself. Therefore, Jesus' question is a challenge that prompts us to probe our own preconceptions, our assumptions, our labels. We cannot reduce Jesus to what we would like him to be. For if we do not know Jesus as he is, then we cannot love him as he is. And if we do not know the true Jesus, then we cannot truly know ourselves.

That is why, in giving our response, we discover the answer to another very important question: Who do we think that we are? Only Jesus Christ can reveal to us who we truly are. For if we were to search the sum total of human ideas, memories, actions, and attitudes then we would come up with a truly pathetic picture of the human being. Only Christ can reveal the true beauty and dignity of the human person, and he does so by inviting us to discover who he is.

It is Peter who makes the declaration: "You are the Messiah." But what does he mean by such an assertion? To claim that Jesus is the Messiah requires that we give up our mistaken ideas about happiness, power, and salvation. The high priest who interrogates Jesus and the people who

115

taunt him on the cross possess a deficient understanding of the Messiah (Mk 14:61, 15:32). So crucial is this need that Jesus rebukes Peter for trying to hold him back. For to assess the graces of heaven by human standards is nothing short of satanic.

However, once we know the truth about Jesus' Messiahship, then we can fully embrace the truth about ourselves. That is why the next thing that Jesus does is "summon the crowd" and inform them of the three prerequisites for discipleship. Without holy self-forgetfulness we end up remembering things about ourselves that only lead us away from Christ. Despite its arduousness, we take up the cross of Jesus in order to be saved from taking on things that would otherwise destroy us. And we follow in Jesus' footsteps to avoid pursuing our own damning will and whim. No matter what we lose in the process, we end up gaining Jesus Christ our life.

Twenty-Fifth Sunday in Ordinary Time

The School of Evangelization
Mark 9:30-37

As Jesus descends from the mountain where he has been transfigured and when he has expelled a demon from the possessed boy, he begins a journey through Galilee. Curiously, he does not want anyone to know about it. For this journey prepares and forms his disciples to be true evangelizers — proclaimers of the Good News.

The first lesson in becoming an evangelizer is the revelation of the Passion: "The Son of Man is to be handed over to men and they will kill him, and three days after his death he will rise." The disciples failed to understand his words, and instead of asking for clarification of the teaching, the disciples became "afraid to question Jesus."

We see this fear at other moments in the Gospel of Mark. The woman with the hemorrhage, whose superstition emboldens her to attempt to steal a healing from Jesus, becomes fearful because Jesus finds her out (Mk 5:33). The disciples who followed behind Jesus on the road to Jerusalem were filled with fear (Mk 10:32). And the chief priest and scribes were afraid of Jesus because the crowds were carried away by Jesus' teaching (Mk 11:18, 12:12). Such fear in Mark is a sign of a weak and deficient faith.

Just as Jesus was transfigured on the mountain, so must this cowering fear be transfigured into the life-giving fear of the Lord. For that holy fear empowers believers to embrace the Passion as God's will with the same love for the Father that inspired Jesus to lay down his life, overcoming every human fear.

The disciples' failure to question Jesus is exacerbated by the silence that falls upon them when Jesus questions them: "What were you arguing about on the way?" In their speechlessness the disciples bear a shameful similarity to the silent Pharisees who refuse to answer the Lord when he asks them if it is permitted to do good, to preserve life on the Sabbath

(Mk 3:4). The disciples' silence masks the guilt they have as a result of arguing about "who was the most important." But the Lord, who has just cast out a mute and deaf demon from the possessed boy, will not permit a similar evil spirit of silence to possess his disciples.

It is true that Jesus also becomes silent. But his silence before the high priest (Mk 14:61) proclaims his rejection of every earthly claim to greatness. And it is that submission to God's will, that devotion to service, and that emptying of self that make the silence of Christian rectitude pure. The one who wants to rank first must remain last and become the servant of all. True humility espouses silence out of reverence, not regret. For in recollected silence, the Christian contemplates the opportunities for giving service to others — service that is the outward expression of the loving union with Jesus which is the source of the Christian's greatness.

And true disciples of the Gospel must be childlike. For without the disposition of a child, we lack receptivity to Jesus in our midst. Therefore, we must "welcome a child such as this" first in ourselves. That bearing in turn makes us responsive to the littleness, the vulnerability, the neediness of others. We see their need as an invitation to respond to the Father's love with generosity. And we do that by sharing with others the love of Jesus that becomes ours through our union with his Passion, with dynamic humility, as adopted sons and daughters of God.

Twenty-Sixth Sunday in Ordinary Time

Learning Our Name in Jesus
Mark 9:38-43, 45, 47-48

What does it mean to be "of the company" of Jesus? As today's Gospel makes clear, it begins in professing the Holy Name of Jesus. Jesus prevents his disciples from trying to stop the man who is using Jesus' name to expel demons. He gives this reason: "No one who performs a mighty deed in my name who can at the same time speak ill of me."

By this action, the Lord confirms the sacredness of every person's name. For our name acts as an icon of our person — an icon that honors the personal dignity that our name signifies. This is true first and foremost of the Holy Name of Jesus. It is by revealing the Holy Name of Jesus — first to Mary and Joseph, and then to the world — that God manifests his holiness so as to restore men and women to his divine image.

Since Jesus united himself to all people through his Incarnation, all people can invoke his Holy Name. Jesus' name expresses both his identity and his mission. It is the way that the Lord makes himself known to others, that he hands himself over and becomes accessible to people, personally and intimately, beginning with the believer who embraces the Holy Name.

This reliance on the Holy Name of Jesus remains far more vital than other aspects of our life that we might otherwise consider essential — like parts of our body. The Holy Name of Jesus puts us in contact with the Person of Christ. Anything that keeps us from ultimate communion with the Person of Christ, that is, anything that impedes our entrance into the Kingdom of God, is to be severed and separated from us. What remains essential for true holiness is the wholeness of our person as it is formed and perfected by the Person of Christ.

The man who gives a Christian a drink "because you belong to Christ" will not go without his reward precisely because he honors the Person of Christ in the bodily needs of the believer. His work of mercy manifests a spiritual depth and sensitivity that manifest reverence for a higher law of love. Conversely, those who spiritually abuse "simple believers" by leading them astray can expect the worst kind of punishment, a punishment that makes being plunged into the sea with a millstone fastened around the neck seem mild. The Lord's strong words signal his infinite love for the divine image alive in every person.

Jesus reveals that we have the power to prepare ourselves for eternal life. Sanctity consists, not in the perfection of our bodies, but in the soundness of our souls. In this Gospel, Jesus is not advocating mutilation, but calling us to find our completeness in Christ. The gift of freedom empowers us to make choices and to reorder our priorities so that we live, not by our own name, but by the Name of Jesus.

As long as we claim the Name of Jesus as our own, we need not fear the loss of our hand, eye, or foot. For the same Lord who healed the shriveled hand of the man in the synagogue, who restored sight to the eyes of the blind man, and who washed the feet of his disciples, provides even more for us as he calls us to the Eucharist by name.

Twenty-Seventh Sunday in Ordinary Time

The Sacrament of Marriage and Our Union With Christ
Mark 10:2-16

"[Some] Pharisees approached and asked 'Is it lawful for a husband to divorce his wife?' They were testing him." Their test involves pitting Jesus against Moses. But it really attempts to promote the authority of the lawgiver over that of the Eternal Word of God Incarnate. And in this way the joke is on the Pharisees. For their bone of contention is, ironically, the very heart of Christ's mission as man: Jesus has come that all may be one, even as he is one with his Father. The Lord effects that oneness by bringing about a union between himself and the Church, a union that is signified in the sacrament of marriage.

In their obstinacy to adhere to convenient customs and standards, the Pharisees have blindly overlooked how the coming of Christ ushers in a completely New Order. The New Order of Christ fulfills and perfects the order of things established by the Creator. And it is an order that anyone can understand through the use of human reason. That is why the Lord's articulate reply is eloquent in its simplicity and reasonableness.

For this New Order also extends to the sacrament of marriage that Christ establishes. The sacrament of marriage introduces people into an ecclesial order that obliges them to certain rights and duties within the Church. First and foremost, marriage commits husbands and wives to protecting and perfecting that perpetual and exclusive bond of love created in marriage through the grace of Christ.

To believe the marital bond can be broken is to assert that God's love for us can come to an end. For the divine power that binds husband and wife is the same power that binds the Church to Christ. Jesus commands, "What God has joined together, no human being must separate." For to attempt to dissolve the indissoluble bond of marriage is to attempt to sever the very unity of God.

Only a heart given over to the New Order of Christ can benefit from the graces flowing from the Church's sacramental order. Moses wasn't able to change the people's hearts. Rather, he accommodated their stubbornness by writing the divorce commandment for them when they refused to relinquish their "hardness of heart." That same term is used only one other time in the Gospel of Mark, 16:14, where we read that the risen Jesus took the Eleven to task for their disbelief and hardness of heart, since they had put no faith in those who had seen him after he had been raised.

Christ will not allow the compromise that comes from hard-heartedness. Therefore, he purifies our hearts by renewing and refashioning them in the same love that binds him to the Father. That is to say, he makes our hearts like the hearts of children. And he insists that we approach him, without hindrance, as children. For then we rejoice to be rid of every human inclination that seeks separation and division as we are welcomed into the Kingdom of God — that paradise of holy unity symbolized in the Eucharist.

Twenty-Eighth Sunday in Ordinary Time

The Promises in Jesus' Face
Mark 10:17-30

Today's Gospel simmers with pent-up expectations. The wealthy man who has "kept the commandments" from his childhood expects an easy, congratulatory answer to his question: "Good Teacher, what must I do to inherit eternal life?" The Lord replies, "You are lacking in one thing. Go, sell what you have, and give to (the) poor and you will have treasure in heaven; then come, follow me."

The man's response shows unmitigated shock: "At that statement his face fell." So singular is his disappointment that this is the only time the New Testament uses the expression. It suggests that the man's whole personal world has collapsed. And that is just the point. The man's personal world of wealth, security, and self-satisfaction cannot coexist with the everlasting life Christ offers.

Jesus' threefold command reveals the predisposition of grace required of those who would share in everlasting life, a grace that goes against all worldly expectations. The joy of the Kingdom of God cannot be grasped without charity that impels us to a self-donation devoted to the poor, without hope fixed on the treasure in heaven, or without faith that commits us to follow Christ fully. God himself imparts this grace to us, but only if we welcome it. Preoccupation with our own possessions, "virtue," and deficient ideas of sanctity prevents it.

Grace asks us to grapple with the impossible with uncompromising realism, "completely overwhelmed" by our own limitations. For at that moment, the Lord of mercy proclaims to us, "With God all things are possible." But it is only after we have confronted the impossible in our own feeble efforts that we see — and crave — what only God's mercy makes possible.

How crucial it is then to live "with God" and not "in ourselves." With Peter, it remains imperative for us to put aside everything to follow

Christ. That self-emptying saves us from all deceptive self-reliance. And God rewards it with relationships, security, and blessings a hundred times richer because they come from God himself. That partaking of God's own life also involves our sharing in the cross of his Son — the persecution that is our greatest privilege.

And if we have any doubt about these divine promises, all we need to do is gaze into the face of Jesus, who looks at the man — and at us — "with love." In that look we know that even we — when our own face falls — in our poverty, our weakness, and our unworthiness, can be saved.

Notice, though, that Jesus doesn't promise us another father. "No one is good but God alone." And we receive that goodness from the Father of Jesus as we remain united to his Son as he "set[s] out on a journey" to Jerusalem to give up — not his home, or money, or property — but his very life. The Lord who calls us to sell what we have and give to the poor gives up his very Flesh and Blood — the greatest lesson of the Good Teacher that convinces us how blessed are the poor in spirit. And in that spirit, the reign of God, the very goodness of God becomes ours.

Twenty-Ninth Sunday in Ordinary Time

Sharing in God's Glory
Mark 10:35-45

Jesus knows that the privilege of sitting on his right or on his left is not his to give. Nonetheless, he asks James and John: "Can you drink the cup I drink or be baptized with the baptism with which I am baptized?" The question is not meant to lead them on or to build up false expectations. Rather, the question indicates to them and to us what is required to share in Christ's glory. Like Zebedee's sons, at times we too do not know what we are asking. To conceive of Christ's glory outside of personal association with his cross is to distort and cheapen the glory of the Resurrection.

The intention of Jesus is not to place conditions on our sharing in his glory, but rather to maximize it. Any self-promoting striving after glory misses the whole point. The glory of Jesus is union in the Spirit with the resplendence of the Father's love through the perfect fulfillment of his will. Christ attains his glory through his self-emptying sacrifice. When we are too full of self, then we negate our ability to enjoy the communion of the Persons of the Trinity. That's what God's glory means.

Therefore, to share in divine glory isn't a question of geography; it doesn't matter how close we sit to Christ. Instead, it is a matter of fulfilling the responsibilities entrusted to us via the bath of baptism and the cup of the Eucharist. Our Christian vocation, which destines us for glory, calls us at every moment to deeper conversion, conversion first and foremost of our minds. As long as we conceive of glory in some self-aggrandizing way, we make a mockery of Calvary and belittle our human dignity. Worldly standards cannot approach the glory God has in store for us. Are we willing to put our false and misleading notions of glory aside?

The other ten apostles become indignant at the precociousness of James and John. But the right kind of indignation is that which Jesus manifested last week when the disciples wanted to keep the children from approaching him. The childlike spirit is perfectly disposed to divine glory. A misdirected indignation appears later, in Mark 14:3-9, towards the woman who anoints the Lord with expensive perfume. But Jesus extols the woman for her kindness by which, in an anticipated way, she unites herself to his Passion.

The simplicity of the child and the service of the anointing woman sum up by example true greatness which Jesus defines: "Anyone who aspires to greatness must serve the rest; whoever wants to rank first among you must serve the needs of all." However, this is not merely philosophy; it is the recapitulation of Christ's own mission: "The Son of Man did not come to be served but to serve and to give his life as a ransom for many."

Therefore, it is not enough to empty ourselves of self. All authentic self-donation must remain directed toward the Person of Jesus, just as Christ's self-sacrifice is offered to the Father. Sensitive, solicitous service of the needs of others assures us that our heart and mind are fixed on Christ and emptied of seductive self-love that forever beguiles us to put ourselves first.

If the Lord didn't command us to this service, our tainted human condition would never allow us to experience just how glorious and satisfying it is to care for another person without a thought of self.

THIRTIETH SUNDAY IN ORDINARY TIME

SEEING OUR WAY TO JESUS OUR WAY
Mark 10:46-52

There are several similarities in today's Gospel account of blind Bartimaeus to that of the wealthy man found earlier in the same chapter. In both stories, Jesus is setting out on a journey. In both episodes, Jesus stops and alters his schedule so as to consider the petition that each man puts before him.

By his own initiative and power, the wealthy man runs up to Jesus and kneels down before him. But blind Bartimaeus doesn't have that ability. All he can do to get the Lord's attention is call out, "Jesus, son of David, have pity on me!" Even when the crowd scolds him to keep quiet, his tenacity kicks in, and Bartimaeus shouts his request all the louder. Because of the persistence of these cries, "Jesus stopped and said, 'Call him.' "

Notice how it is that Bartimaeus comes to know of the Lord's presence nearby: "on hearing that it was Jesus of Nazareth." Due to his blindness, Bartimaeus relies in a preeminent way on his sense of hearing. Obviously, someone had told Bartimaeus about Jesus and his reputation. What specifically Bartimaeus was told we can never be sure. But one thing is clear: somehow in his mind and heart, Bartimaeus identifies Jesus with the Son of David. That is, Bartimaeus recognizes in Jesus the one who manifests God's fidelity to his promises of a promised land, of happiness and satisfaction, of a new covenant. Bartimaeus "sees" Jesus as the Messiah. And because of this profession of faith and confidence, Christ stops and commands: "Call him."

Bartimaeus' faith is so great that, in response to Jesus' summons, Bartimaeus "threw aside his cloak." Unlike the wealthy man, whose face falls at the prospect of selling all his possessions and giving to the poor, the destitute Bartimaeus willingly gives up his most prized possession, his cloak, in order to be with Jesus. The cloak was the poor person's sole source of warmth, of protection from the elements, and of bedding for night's sleep. Bartimaeus' jumping up and running to Jesus indicate that he seeks all his strength, security, and solace in nothing but the Lord. He believes that Jesus will provide everything needed.

Every Christian longs to hear the question that Jesus puts to Bartimaeus: "What do you want me to do for you?" One suspects that at that moment Bartimaeus could have made the most extravagant demand and be granted it (an ironic echo of Herod's offer in Mark 6:22-25 which was met with treachery). But all Bartimaeus asks of "Rabboni" is to be able to see. Bartimaeus does not ask anything for himself. For, immediately upon receiving his sight, Bartimaeus uses his new gift of vision to follow Jesus up the road. Faith effects his sight; the gift of sight deepens his longing to live by faith.

The wealthy man went away sad, but Bartimaeus went on the Way who is Jesus himself. And just as Jesus relies on disciples in his service to call Bartimaeus to him, Bartimaeus — and we — are called to use our gift of faith-vision to recognize those on the roadside in need of the Messiah's pity, and to bring them to Jesus.

Thirty-First Sunday in Ordinary Time

The Divine Priority of Love
Mark 12:28-34

What did the scribe expect Jesus to say when he asked him: "Which is the first of all the commandments?" What would we consider the first? Scrupulously obeying all the rules? Giving God groveling submission? Committing oneself to being a good person possessed of the right values? Clearly, the answer that Jesus gave was not the one that the scribe had in mind. Nor is it what many might rank as first.

The first commandment is not to obey God, nor to revere God, nor to respect God like some reliable role model. Rather, the first commandment is to *love* God, and to love him with every excellent faculty of our personal existence. If we do not love God with all our heart, then it becomes hardened (Mk 3:5, 16:14) — the source of all destructive evil (Mk 7:21). If we do not love God with all our soul, then we lack the resilience to withstand our own agony in the garden (Mk 14:34). If we do not love God with all our mind, then we will consider those who do so to be out of their mind (Mk 3:21). And if we do not love God with all our strength, then we will use our power to indulge every end of unhealthy self-love.

However, the scribe clearly regards Christ's pronouncement as both an innovation and an improvement. It leads him to repeat all of Jesus' words in a kind of public profession of faith. For the scribe recognizes that we cannot have any other *modus operandi* in life but love. God brings into existence, permeates, and infuses every single dimension of human life. He is the love that fills our heart; he is the life that quickens our soul; he is the truth that enlightens our mind; he is the way that makes us strong. To refuse to love God, first and fully, is to attempt to place God outside our life, as if we possess some way to exist and to excel without him. Such thinking constitutes the deadly sin of idolatry.

Only love keeps us from such prideful presumption. The scribe asserts this when he declares that love of God and neighbor "is worth more than all burnt offerings and sacrifices." In other words, authentic love far surpasses any human initiative, any effort to rely on our own resources, any attempt to get by merely appeasing God. Plenty of sacrifices could easily be offered without a shred of affection. But when we love God above all else then we honor and cherish him in a way that surpasses every other because then we worship God for who he is: Love.

Jesus approves the scribe's answer because the scribe is using his fine mind, not to penetrate the subtle theological intricacies of Christ's proposition, but to *love God*. He is not far from the reign of God because he is using his mind, not merely to understand, but to love God wholly.

No one had the courage to ask Jesus any more questions. The only other time this word is used in Mark is in the description of Joseph of Arimathea boldly asking Pilate for the body of Jesus (Mk 15:43). The people lack the courage to question Jesus further because they are not daring enough to make love the priority of their life. But the example of Joseph shows us that such daring love of God blesses us with the courage to love Jesus and each other even unto death.

Thirty-Second Sunday in Ordinary Time

Humility, Poverty, and True Generosity
Mark 12:38-44

Jesus has come to Jerusalem to lay down his life. As he teaches in the temple, he warns against scribes who accept "seats of honor in the synagogues," and who "devour the [savings] of widows." Jesus then proceeds to take a seat and to observe the almsgiving of a widow.

Christ's seat-taking stands in radical contrast to the self-seeking motives of the scribes. Jesus takes a seat when he teaches the Twelve about what it means to rank first: childlike lowliness and a humble willingness to serve (Mk 9:35). When Jesus cleanses the temple, he overturns the seats of the pigeon sellers because they represent an attempt to purchase God's favor. The seat he takes at this moment foreshadows the request he will make of his apostles as he enters into his agony: "Sit here while I pray" (Mk 14:32). This is the only sitting that truly honors God and that gains glory for ourselves. It is fulfilled in the Ascension when the Lord Jesus "was taken up into heaven and took his seat at the right hand of God" (Mk 16:19).

From his seated position, like a good pastor, Jesus oversees the collection. There Jesus takes note of one poor widow. In instructing the rich man on the requirements for discipleship, Jesus alludes to the poor: "Go, sell what you have, and give to (the) poor" (Mk 10:21). A definite contrast is set up between this poor widow and the rich man. The rich man fails to follow Jesus because there is one thing he lacks; the poor widow stands as a true disciple because she gave from her need. As he enters his Passion, Jesus will say about the woman who anoints his feet, "the poor you will always have with you" (Mk 14:7). The poor remain a consistent part of God's Providence because they show us the right way to trust and to abandon ourselves to divine compassion.

The greatest thing that we can give to God is the gift of our very selves motivated by the same love with which God loves us. Anything offered to God out of pure, unmitigated, heartfelt love constitutes a greater contribution than something given simply from surplus. We are told that the poor widow "contributed all she had, her whole livelihood." The term used is the word for life. In her own way, the widow's offering represents the Christ-like act of laying down her life. She gives of herself, utterly and without limit, not out of a sense of self-importance, not in order to win the praise of her peers, not in order get anything for herself, but simply because she believes in God. The authenticity of her love and belief is demonstrated in her sacred desire to give totally of herself. It is not the amount of her donation, but rather the ardor of her love that makes her offering the most precious.

Sinful people desire to devour the savings of widows. But when we freely and completely give ourselves to God, then God gives us himself to eat in the Eucharist. His life is what we have to live on.

THIRTY-THIRD SUNDAY IN ORDINARY TIME

LIVING IN THE LIGHT
Mark 13:24-32

The end of the liturgical year reminds us of the approach of the end of the world at the Second Coming of Christ. Jesus describes how it will be a time of utter darkness: "But in those days, after that tribulation, the sun will be darkened, and the moon will not give its light, and the stars will be falling from the sky, and the powers in the heavens will be shaken."

However, the Lord goes on to explain: "And then they will see 'the Son of Man' coming in the clouds with great power and glory." But if all the natural sources of light have been extinguished, by what light will people be able to see Christ's coming? By the light who is Christ the Light, the light of the world.

In order to avoid fear and trembling when darkness prevails at the end of time, Christ calls us to live in his light right now. Today's Gospel shows us three ways. It means, first of all, living a sacramental life, that is, being attentive and united to all the sacred signs around us that bespeak and bestow divine life. Jesus counsels us to "learn a lesson from the fig tree" whose sprouting leaves signal the coming of summer.

Two chapters previously, the Lord curses a fig tree in Jerusalem because it lacks fruit. The next morning, when Peter discovers the fig tree withered to its roots, he expresses his astonishment. Jesus replies: "Have faith in God." In the sacraments the Lord has left us efficacious signs that continue to impart God's saving action. The more we put our trust in them, the better we are prepared for the final coming of Christ.

True preparation for Christ's coming also means giving primacy to Jesus' words. In chapter eight, the Lord warns: "Whoever is ashamed of me and of my words in this faithless and sinful generation, the Son of Man will be ashamed of when he comes in his Father's glory with the holy angels" (Mk 8:38). Therefore, living by Jesus' words must remain a supreme priority in our life. As the Lord promises in the Gospel of John:

133

"Whoever hears my word . . . has eternal life. . . . Whoever keeps my word will never see death. . . . Whoever loves me will keep my word, and my Father will love him, and we will come to him and make our dwelling with him" (Mk 5:24, 8:51, 14:23). That is why the Lord is bold to declare today that "Heaven and earth will pass away, but my words will not pass away."

And preparation for the Second Coming means living as a true child of God. Jesus explains that no one knows the exact day or hour — "only the Father." This isn't a threat but an invitation to greater intimacy with God. If the Father is the only one who knows when the end is coming, then logically it makes sense to stay as close to the Father as we can. We must live in alert expectation, but as children of God. That is why Jesus teaches us to pray "Our Father." Then, in a spirit of holy openness, dependency, and docility, we're not anxious about the end. We remain confident that we will be one of the chosen that God's angels assemble "from the ends of earth and to the end of the sky." That election begins today as the Lord calls us to Holy Communion.

CHRIST THE KING SUNDAY

CLAIMING THE KINGSHIP OF CHRIST
John 18:33b-37

Pontius Pilate asks Jesus: "Are you the King of the Jews?" And the Lord responds: "Do you say this on your own or have others told you about me?" In other words, the Lord reveals his kingship, not to those who approach with idle curiosity, but to those who are willing to commit themselves in faith to Christ and to the truth he reveals.

Pilate's reply reveals far more than it seems. He says: "I am not a Jew, am I?" In the Gospel of John, the term "the Jews" does not refer to any racial or ethnic group. Rather, the term signifies all those who reject the revelation of divine truth in Jesus Christ. Therefore, in claiming "I am not a Jew," Pilate ironically indicates — without knowing it — that he is open to the truth manifested in Christ the King. For the careful reader, Pilate's response hints at the unfailing hope that the Good News offers again and again, even up to the moment of Jesus' death.

Jesus asserts: "You say I am a king." To know the kingship of Christ, we must claim Christ as King. And we do that in three ways. First, to claim Christ as King we must refuse to set our hearts or desires on the world, because "my kingdom does not belong to this world." As long as we rely on worldly standards, insights, and expectations then we will remain mired in Pilate's muddle. The Kingdom of Christ is that gathering of people around Jesus Christ who have been raised up to share in the Father's divine life. It is a grace that begins on earth, but that is ultimately fulfilled in heaven. That is why, in claiming Christ as King, we keep our hearts and our minds fixed on what is above.

Second, to claim Christ as King is to accept and reverence the motives for the Incarnation: "For this I was born and for this I came into the world, to testify to the truth." The truth to which Christ testifies is the truth of the Father's merciful love and the tragic truth of the human need for salvation due to sin. We cannot share in the kingship of Christ if we do not admit the truth about ourselves: if we do not acknowledge our sinfulness and turn it over to our Savior King in heartfelt contrition. The reason why Christ's would-be subjects fail to fight to save Jesus from his enemies is that they are fighting their own private demons, and losing. As long as we allow ourselves to remain subjected to sin, then Christ's death on the cross becomes meaningless. We reject every impulse to save Jesus from death as long as we deny our own need for salvation.

And to claim Christ as King means to hear his voice and to heed his words in testimony that we are committed to the truth. God's will and the authority of Jesus remain the driving forces of our life. Pilate cannot recognize Christ as King until he is willing to abdicate his own earthly authority.

Pilate asks Jesus, "What have you done?" And as we approach Christ the King in the Eucharist, we know that the answer is, "More than anyone can say."

PART TWO:
REFLECTIONS ON
SOLEMNITIES AND FEASTS
THAT MAY FALL ON
SUNDAY

IMMACULATE CONCEPTION

HOW TO CONCEIVE OF THE IMMACULATE CONCEPTION
Luke 1:26-38

The Immaculate Conception is that magnificent moment when God's tender love pierces the pall of human sinfulness by raising up a creature untouched by the scourge of sin — a woman destined to mediate God's love to us as a mother.

The angel suggests Mary's privileged distinction of being without original sin in the greeting he utters. The angel enjoins Mary to "rejoice." The Blessed Virgin Mary is the preeminent person in the world capable of rejoicing, for joy is the elation we experience when our will desires something ordered to our true happiness and when we possess that desired good. Because Mary's Immaculate Heart remains wholly conformed and devoted to the will of God, everything that she desires is a manifestation of the divine will. As a result, Mary can truly rejoice. In fact, her very life is an act of rejoicing, for every act of her sinless will stands as the human fulfillment of the will of God: her only desire.

In some translations, the angel calls Mary "O highly favored daughter." In other words, it is as if the Father himself is speaking to Mary as his child. Obviously, Mary's "high favor" has nothing to do with Mary's talents, virtues, or merits apart from God. Rather, Mary is called highly favored and is highly favored precisely because she is God's daughter. The goodness that Mary possesses from the moment of her Immaculate Conception is solely the fruit of her relationship with God. The Father's love, the Father's preference, the Father's initiative makes Mary highly favored. Her favor has nothing to do with anything she has done on her own. God himself, in the person of the angel, acknowledges Mary's Immaculate favor *so that we will learn to do the same.*

The angel next asserts: "The Lord is with you." This doesn't mean merely that Mary is close to God. Rather, it indicates God's divine presence indwelling in Mary with special power. Jesus himself will use a similar expression at the Last Supper when he says to his apostles: "I have earnestly desired to eat this Passover with you before I suffer" (Lk 22:15).

Jesus desires to be one with his apostles in Holy Communion so that the Lord will be with them at that moment in the way that transforms the world forever. In Mary's Immaculate Conception, that divine efficacy is already at work.

And finally, the angel declares: "Blessed are you among women." Mary is blessed with the blessedness that Jesus promises to those who live the Beatitudes. Mary's Immaculate Conception is a living embodiment of the fullness of the Beatitudes.

The angel says all these things to the Blessed Virgin Mary *before* she conceives Jesus in her womb, and they are recounted in the Gospel *for us*. The Immaculate Conception shows us that real joy is possible in our life when we let Mary help us unite our will to God's. The Immaculate Conception liberates us from seeking high favor in anything else but the privilege of being God's children.

Mary our Immaculate Mother makes that relationship possible. The Immaculate love of Mary assures us of God's closeness and intimacy when we feel farthest from him. When we, like the apostles, find ourselves on the verge of betrayal, our renewed devotion to the Immaculate Conception rescues us from the horror of being left to ourselves instead of with God. And the Immaculate Conception saves us from worldly deceptions about what constitutes "blessedness." We find that blessedness in our life in the same way that God finds Mary today: by calling out with heartfelt devotion to Mary the Immaculate Conception.

CHRISTMAS

BEGINNING A NEW BEGINNING
John 1:1-18

Christmas is a new beginning, a fresh opportunity to renew our relationship with God. "In the beginning" of this beginning is the Word who is God. And because this Word is first and foremost both in creation and Christmas, the celebration of the Incarnation calls us to put aside all the other lesser "words" that we live by. Jesus the Word is born to be the principle, the priority, the pinnacle of our lives. He is the only Word that really matters. As long as our hearts and minds remain cluttered with other ideas, opinions, judgments, and convictions, then Christmas comes upon us as just another meaningless day. To welcome Christmas means to put aside every self-centered notion that keeps us from accepting God's gift of his Son. The Father speaks his Word at Christmas to fill our lives with true meaning and peace.

"All things came to be through him, and without him nothing came to be." Our very existence is an expression of the miracle of Christmas. We were created in Christ. As a result, any attempt to make sense of our life outside of Christ is to step back into the chaotic void that creation undid. In this first chapter of the Gospel, John asserts: "Without him nothing came to be." And the night before he dies, Jesus declares: "Without me you can do nothing" (Jn 15:5). We cannot exist apart from the creative power of Christ. And we can enjoy no true success or achievement in life apart from the redemptive sacrifice of Christ.

Christmas, then, is God's challenge to give up our prideful, self-generating ways, and to permit ourselves to be "begotten by God." This new identity, this new way of being becomes ours as soon as we stop living by some name that we falsely hope to make for ourselves, and we start believing in the name of Jesus. Christmas calls us to cling to that Name with the same urgency with which we would save our life. Because it is our Life.

"What came to be through him was life, and this life was the light of the human race." The Gospel assures us that "the light shines in the darkness." But in order to appreciate the life-giving power of the light, we must first admit that we live enshrouded in darkness. Otherwise, we turn away from the light fearful that it will further blind us. The first step to true enlightenment is acknowledging our need for a light that does not come from ourselves. When we come to be in Jesus, instead of remaining holed up in ourselves, then we rejoice to see God's light shining on the darkness of our sinfulness, our selfishness, our self-righteousness, our haughtiness.

The more we own up to our self-imposed darkness, the more the graces of Christmas become our own. Then, in the wondrous new beginning of Christmas, we are one with the Word, we are united in God's presence, and we are like God himself. And then the great beginning of Christmas assures us of our place in the joyful ending of the Resurrection.

The Presentation of the Lord

The Goodness That Comes to Those Who Wait
Luke 2:22-40

Only a few weeks ago, on the feast of the Holy Family, we heard this same Gospel proclaimed. But we meditate upon it again today to celebrate the new manifestation of Jesus as Messiah as he is presented in the temple.

Simeon and Anna represent all of us who have been waiting and searching for the Lord in order to find in him the ultimate meaning of our life. In this way, they embody the theological virtue of hope, living in confidence with their souls fixed on the promises of God. What enables them to pick this child out of the crowd and to acclaim him as the Anointed of the Lord? If we can answer that question then we too can share in the transforming graces offered in the mystery of the Presentation.

First of all, we are told that Simeon and Anna were waiting in the temple, which means they were waiting in holiness. So often, when our life lacks focus, purpose, direction, or fulfillment, we entertain the temptation to dissipation, worldliness, materialism, etc. God has his reasons for not answering all our prayers as immediately as we might desire. One reason aims to purify and strengthen our desires so as to conform them more perfectly to what God wants for us.

Simeon and Anna's prolonged period of sanctified waiting prepares them to partake with great joy in all the richness of the Presentation. Their God-centered patience refines their perseverance and perception so that they settle for nothing less than God in their lives. Holiness is their tutor. Simeon and Anna readily welcome God's Son in the temple because they have first nurtured godliness in their own lives.

But something else disposes them profoundly to see in the Christ-child "a light for revelation to the Gentiles." Simeon's and Anna's lives have both been formed by suffering. Simeon is presented to us with all the virtues of a monk. He has lived his life in complete self-donation to God, with unfailing dedication and utter detachment. His life remains focused on his death: the moment when God's anointed would be revealed to him. And this delights him and gives him great peace.

143

In the same way, Anna's life is marked by constant asceticism. She has lived perhaps fifty or sixty years alone as a widow, fasting, consumed by prayer. And because both of these holy ones value the redemptive power of sacrifice in their relationship with God, they are quick to receive the Holy One of God as he is consecrated in the temple with a sacrifice.

And finally, Simeon's esteem for Mary opens his eyes to the presence of Jesus. In fact, the Presentation is depicted as another version of the Visitation. The Mother of God who once bore Jesus in her womb to Elizabeth now caries her child into the temple where Simeon takes him in his arms. At the prospect of giving birth to her Son, Mary sings her *Magnificat* in Elizabeth's house. Now at the fulfillment of God's Word in the "saving deed displayed for all the peoples to see" — the Incarnation — it is Simeon who sings his canticle in the temple. And Anna joins in the glory and the joy by giving thanks to God and talking about the child to all. The Mother of God, who presents her Son to God and to us, also enables us to embrace the graces that continue to flow to us through the Presentation.

St. Joseph, the Husband of Mary

How to Love Jesus in Mary
Matthew 1:16, 18-21, 24

The Church honors St. Joseph twice in the liturgical year: in the month of May as the worker, and today as the husband of Mary. Why would the Church solemnly celebrate the fact that a particular man was married? Because Joseph's marriage provides us the model and the means for us to love Mary, and to love Jesus as Joseph and Mary love him.

We must not overlook the fact that the story of Christmas — the story of salvation — begins with a sorrow of truly tragic proportions. Matthew tells us that the birth of Jesus Christ came about as a consequence of the broken heart of Joseph. When Joseph found Mary with child, he experienced a sorrow perhaps too great for us to fathom. Joseph would have to give up his beloved Mary. The fact that Joseph was severely grieved at the thought of losing Mary is proved in the way he decided to "divorce her quietly." Joseph could have raged and wailed and denounced the cause of his presumably ruined life. But the depth and integrity of Joseph's love for Mary is demonstrated in his noble, suffering response. In his mind, Joseph must have thought that Mary was in love with someone else. And in a way he was right. But Joseph loved Mary too much to interfere with Mary's heart or to do anything to hurt her, despite the hurt he must have felt.

Joseph's pain was necessary. Because of his suffering, Joseph was prepared to love Mary even more than the strength of his human heart. Joseph's hurt opened his heart to the message of the angel. His trial disposed Joseph to see that there was much more to his bride than the human beauty, virtue, and goodness he found in her; now Joseph could see that Mary was filled with God's life. Joseph could love Mary as God's own love. In choosing Mary to be his wife, Joseph chose God to be his life.

Joseph was not only to marry Mary. The angel commands him: "You are to name [the child] Jesus." In this way, Joseph becomes a true father to Jesus. He gives his Son his true identity, an identity that comes from heaven but is revealed to the world through the paternal love of Joseph.

The child is to be named Jesus "because he will save his people from their sins." Joseph will teach his Son about human sinfulness by showing him how much he himself avoids it by his devout life of faith, hope, and love. Jesus learns obedience — learns when and how to obey the Father's will — through what he suffers. Jesus learns that obedience especially by observing the way that Joseph suffers out of his love for God and out of his desire to do only what God asks of him.

Ever since the appearance of the angel in his dream, every time Joseph thought of Mary he thought of Jesus. Whenever Joseph looked at Mary, he saw Jesus. Mary was the way that Joseph came to know and love Jesus the way he deserves to be known and loved.

"When Joseph awoke he did as the angel of the Lord had commanded him." This feast calls us to awaken and to do what the Lord directs us: to love Mary as Joseph does so that we might truly love Jesus. That is the most fitting way to honor the silent, obedient Joseph.

The Annunciation

Accepting the Mother of God, Accepting Redemption
Luke 1:26-38

The message of the angel announces to Mary that she is to conceive the Savior, and the account in the Gospel announces to us how we are to receive the Savior: through Mary. Since Mary has found favor with God, God makes Mary a special instrument of salvation.

Of all the countless spectacular methods that God could have elected to redeem the world, God chooses a means as mundane and ordinary as childbirth. The revelation of the aged Elizabeth's pregnancy affirms that "nothing [is] impossible with God." And yet, God will not resort to stupendous theophanies in order to inaugurate salvation. Rather, he offers humanity redemption through the phenomenon of motherhood. For, in this way, God not only saves his people, but he blesses them with an unending reminder of why he wants to save us. God offers us salvation, not out of anger, frustration, or exasperation, but only because he loves us. The tenderness, intimacy, and personal consent integral to motherhood perpetually signify the quality and depth of love that move God to save us from the death of sin.

The angel's very explicit message is really meant to penetrate our hearts. The angel declares: "You will conceive." New life will come from a woman who has not "known man." By uniting ourselves to this mystery we are assured that divine life will be born from the seemingly impossible and desperate dimensions of our life. Mary is willing to conceive of Jesus in her womb — "May it be done to me according to your word" — because Mary already conceives of God's goodness, mercy, and wisdom in her mind and heart. The Annunciation calls us to open our hearts to that same kind of conception, leaving our old and ungodly conceptions of the way things are behind.

The angel asserts: "You will bear a Son." His words do not refer merely to the physical birth of Jesus. Rather, Mary will become the Mother of the Person of Christ. Mary's maternal role continues from the moment of Jesus' birth to the present. The life that Mary bears continues to be born in our own life through her maternal mediation. Mary's womb remains ever fruitful so that we might become persons truly configured in holiness and grace to the divine Person of Christ.

And the angel informs Mary: "You shall name him Jesus." Why doesn't the angel let the mother choose a name on her own for her son? Because the Name of Jesus signifies his divine essence and his earthly mission. Mary continues to offer to us the heavenly gift of the Name once conferred on her Son. Mary constantly gives us the Name of Jesus so that we might embrace everything that that name means and effects, and so that we might make Jesus' Name our own: we are first and foremost "Christians." We rely on the Mother of God to claim us as her children and lovingly to speak the Name of Jesus to us in our sorrow and distress.

In saving us, the Lord asks us to accept in our life God's own Maidservant who is also our Mother. When we accept the Blessed Virgin Mary in this way, then we let God's redemption be done in us as he says.

THE ASCENSION

THE ELEVATING POWER OF THE BODY OF CHRIST
Mark 16:15-20

Just before Jesus goes up into the heavens, he commands the Eleven to "Go into the whole world and proclaim the gospel to every creature." Christ's going up into heaven in the Ascension assures that the apostles' going forth to evangelize will be effective and successful.

The question that confronts us as we ponder this mystery is why doesn't Jesus remain on earth after the Resurrection? Why does the Lord have to ascend into heaven? And the answer is that it is only after Christ departs from his disciples physically that they receive a new and deeper share in the Father's love. This love calls every disciple to a new way of relating to the Blessed Trinity, a new way of loving God. If Jesus never ascended, the disciples would content themselves with their old way of knowing and loving God. Christ must leave their sight so as to prepare us for the gift of the Spirit.

This is why Jesus informs his Eleven: "Whoever believes and is baptized will be saved." In other words, Jesus ascends so that others may live by faith. And the world comes to live by faith through the preaching of the apostles — through the preaching of the Church, the visible Body of Christ on earth.

Jesus ascends to the other world of heaven so that his apostles may become otherworldly. The Gospel tells us that "the Lord worked through them and confirmed the word through accompanying signs." Although the body of Jesus is taken from their sight, the world continues to witness to the power of Christ's body in the bodies of the apostles. Jesus promises that five signs will accompany those who have professed their faith: they will expel demons through the utterance of the Holy Name, they will speak new languages, they will handle serpents, they will drink poison, they will heal the sick through the laying on of hands. In other words, through the lips, the tongues, the hands, and the digestive systems of the apostles, the glory of Jesus Christ and the Gospel will continue to be revealed.

Once Jesus ascends into the heavens, all his disciples fix their hearts and minds on what is above. As Christ ascends, so too do our thoughts, needs, and desires ascend to be one with Jesus, who elevates every dimension of our earthly life so as to make it worthy of eternal union with him. The Lord Jesus "took his seat at the right hand of God." Earlier, James and John had asked Christ to: "Grant that in your glory we may sit one at your right and the other at your left" (Mk 10:37). As Jesus ascends into heaven, in a certain respect their request is granted. The apostles share in the ruling power that Christ takes up as he is taken up into heaven to take his seat at the Father's right hand as the Eleven go forth and preach everywhere.

THE BIRTH OF JOHN THE BAPTIST

THE BIRTHDAY THAT HERALDS OUR REBIRTH
Luke 1:57-66, 80

It is somewhat rare for the Church to honor the birthday of the saints. Why do we celebrate the birth — and later the beheading — of John the Baptist? What is so special about his birth for our life of faith?

The attending neighbors and relatives of Zechariah and Elizabeth give us a clue, for they interpret the birth of John as a sign "that the Lord had shown his great mercy." The birth of John is not merely a human marvel but a divine act. The fear that "came upon all their neighbors" is the first stirring of the fear of the Lord that leads to wisdom. "All those who heard these things took them to heart, saying 'What then, will this child be?' " In the same way, the birth of John the Baptist fills our hearts with the grace to receive the coming of Jesus Christ. The birth of John prepares us to reborn as children of God in Christ. As we ask "what will this child be?" we are given an insight into what we will be.

These same neighbors voice their protest when Elizabeth informs them: "He will be called John." In fact, the neighbors intended to name him after his father Zechariah — a somewhat presumptuous intention since it seems to usurp the rights of the parents. Perhaps they thought they were doing well, but it was imperative for the child to be given the name the angel had revealed. For John's name announces his mission in salvation. Even in his infancy, before John the Baptist can speak, he prepares the world to receive Jesus Christ by virtue of his God-given name.

The giving of John's name opens Zechariah's mouth and loosens his tongue. They say that silence is the father of preachers. Once the preacher John is named, his father raises his newly restored voice "blessing God." Zechariah has spent his silent retreat meditating on the meaning of the son to be born to him. John's birth renews Zechariah's — and our — relationship with God. The more that we reflect on the subtlety and intricacy of God's mercy as it is manifested in the birth of John the Baptist, the more we appreciate the birth of Jesus at Christmas.

We need John's birth to rid our hearts of the hardness, the preconceptions, and the doubts that seep into our life of faith. The adamancy shown regarding John's proper name reminds us that our true name, our true identity can only be found in God. For that, we need to listen and to refuse to give in to the usurping pressures of the world, and to let God be our Father. Our voices remain a gift from God to give praise to God in every thought we think and word we speak. We celebrate the birth of John with the fullness of our faith in the hope that, as his birthday gift to us, John the Baptist will help us to be effective like him in preparing others to welcome Christ in their lives.

Saints Peter and Paul

The Grace of Confessing Christ
Matthew 16:13-19

On this feast of the great apostles Peter and Paul, the Gospel focuses our attention on the "confession" of Peter at Caesarea Philippi. For the greatness of all apostles is rooted in their coming to know and to profess Jesus as "the Messiah . . . the Son of the living God."

This knowledge is a supreme gift: "Blessed are you, Simon son of Jonah. For flesh and blood has not revealed this to you, but my heavenly Father." Therefore, we marvel at the sensitive openness of Peter towards God which enables Peter to receive this blessed revelation from the Father. We know how this moment marks a turning point in the faith of Peter. We recall the scene early in the Gospel of Luke when, after the miraculous catch of fish, Peter cries out: "Depart from me, Lord, for I am a sinful man" (Lk 5:8). This episode suggests that Peter's struggle with sin and self-knowledge has brought him to the sanctified knowledge of God's mercy and majesty.

The same is true of Paul. His original obstinacy towards the Christian faith went as far as persecuting the Church. But when Jesus reveals himself to Paul on the road to Damascus, Paul is able to accept him because he first sees the truth about himself. That conversion is symbolized by the scales that blind the eyes of Paul — scales that are removed once Paul enters into the embrace of the Church.

Therefore, as we celebrate the Church's great apostles today, we are reminded of the greatness to which we are called. And yet, we realize that greatness in our lives only if first we humbly acknowledge our own emptiness and weakness before God.

Christ reveals man to himself. In order to answer the Lord's critical question, "Who do people say that the Son of Man is?" we must be willing to acknowledge who Christ is revealing ourselves to be. We can be guaranteed that, no matter the particulars of what Christ reveals to us, our identity in Christ will point to our inescapable need for Jesus to be our

Messiah. Christ reveals the truth of our imperfection to us only to inspire our trust and confidence in his infinite desire to heal us, to elevate us, to transform us, to sanctify us, to save us.

This explains the magnificent promises Christ makes to his apostle. As weak as he may feel, because of Jesus, Peter will remain forever the "Rock." As we unite ourselves to this Rock, the foundation of the Church, we will never be assailed by the sins and weaknesses that seek to undo us. "The powers of death shall not prevail" against the Church. But for those who profess the divinity of Jesus Christ, the Church is not simply a place of refuge from evil. Rather, the Church is a true home, a place of creativity and regeneration. Because of the faith-filled knowledge that convicts the apostle Peter, Christ entrusts to him the keys of the Kingdom of heaven. Who better to administer the divine mercy of the Trinity than the one who throws himself upon that mercy in his most desperate hour?

THE TRANSFIGURATION

SEEING JESUS IN EVERYTHING
Mark 9:2-10

Up to this moment in the Gospel of Mark, the disciples have heard Jesus teach and have seen Jesus heal the sick, expel demons, multiply loaves and fishes, silence raging storms, and walk on water. In just the previous chapter, Peter declares that Jesus is the Messiah (Mk 8:29). Now, as Jesus takes Peter, James, and John off by themselves with him up a "high mountain," those special three must have thought they had a better understanding of Jesus than anyone else. Perhaps they thought they knew Jesus as well as he could be known.

And yet, when they reach the summit, Jesus is transfigured before their eyes. He becomes dazzling white, radiant, luminescent. In fact, Jesus becomes light itself. That is to say, Jesus appears to his apostles as the source of all life on earth, for it is light that gives growth to vegetation, which in turn becomes the food supply for everything that lives. And that is the point of the Transfiguration: Jesus wants his disciples to see him as the source and the summit of everything in their lives. For Jesus is our everything.

We cannot truly appreciate the goodness of anything good in our lives unless we first know and love Jesus Christ, who is the cause of that goodness. Everything has been created *in Christ.* As a result, everything that exists is good and remains a reflection of God's goodness. We need the light of Christ, which is the intimate love of friendship, in order to see and to reverence that reflection. That is what the Transfiguration is all about: seeing Christ as light so as to be able to see everything in our life in the light of Christ. Once we see Jesus like this, we gain a new way of seeing ourselves.

Although the three apostles of this inner circle feel especially close to Jesus, they see that two others are even closer: Elijah and Moses. The apostles have heard very much from Jesus, but it's not certain that they can hear what Elijah and Moses are saying to Jesus. And yet, it is evident that their conversation with Christ is the most important one in the Lord's life. And, naturally, Peter, James, and John — and we — want to be part of it.

Peter knew that it was good to be there, but "he hardly knew what to say," for they were all overcome with awe. For the experience of the Transfiguration made it resplendently clear that there is much more to Jesus than meets the eye. Jesus becomes transfigured before their eyes so that their perception of him might be transfigured. What they see increases their longing to enter into the mystical dialogue they witness. And that is precisely what the overshadowing cloud commands: "Listen to him." To listen to the Son of God we must stop listening to ourselves, to our false loves, to the lies of the world, etc.

Jesus draws them into his most intimate conversation as they come down from the mountain. The Lord reveals that in order to understand the Transfiguration, his disciples must be one with him in his rising from the dead. They continue to discuss privately what "to rise from the dead" means. But as they will discover — and as we know — the true meaning of the Resurrection can be reached only through dying. Therefore, from this moment on, when we look around we will see only Jesus — in our joys, our sufferings, our trials, our hardships, conflicts, and doubts. That's when Transfiguration transfuses us. That's when Jesus Christ becomes our everything.

The Assumption

The Body of Mary and the Body of Christ
Luke 1:39-56

In the Visitation recalled in today's Gospel, the physical, bodily presence of the Blessed Virgin Mary to Elizabeth causes her to be "filled with the holy Spirit." The Assumption of Mary constitutes another kind of Visitation. In the first, Mary bears Jesus in her body to a town of Judah. In the Assumption, Mary's body is borne into heaven so that her physical presence before God might continue to be a cause of the enlivening of the Holy Spirit in all those on earth seeking salvation.

Mary's being "proclaims the greatness of the Lord," and her very body bears the godly greatness that she proclaims. The fact that God assumes Mary bodily into heaven stands as a living indication to us of the all-encompassing fullness of salvation. God's grace transforms and perfects every aspect of our human life. God's mercy is utterly comprehensive, reaching out to elevate and sanctify even our fallen bodies.

Mary proclaims in her *Magnificat* that God "has looked upon his handmaid's lowliness." What is apparent to "look upon" is the seeming lowliness of Mary's body as well as her humble state in life. All ages continue to call Mary blessed in the same way that Mary does: by "looking upon" Mary's lowly body that has been lifted up to the very heights of heaven to signify the unending, transcending force of divine grace.

Mary sings that God "lift[s] up the lowly." As her words come true in her own life on the Assumption, they are meant to be a consolation to us as we struggle with our lowliness. How often do disabilities of our own bodies, either because of age, weight, sickness, disability, injury, bad self-image, etc., get in the way of our relationship with God. God raises Mary to high places to assure us that he longs to do the same to us through the maternal mediation of Mary. The more we reverence Mary lifted up, to her high place with God, the less do we obsess about the weaknesses and deficiencies of our own bodily existence of earth.

"The hungry he has filled with good things." God reveals the power of his saving mercy in a very down-to-earth way: by feeding the bodies of those who hunger for him. To attempt a relationship with God without reference to the role of our own bodies in that friendship is to tempt a kind of dualism: exalting the spiritual to the neglect of the physical. Such errors have repeatedly harmed the Church throughout history.

Therefore, God draws Mary to heaven bodily so that, as we contemplate her with loving devotion, we might realize what ultimate holiness looks like. The characteristics of Christ's body express the Divine Person of the Son of God. In a similar way, the characteristics of Mary's body assumed into heaven express to all her children the genuine image of true sanctity: what it means to be the Body of Christ. The mystery of the Assumption gloriously proclaims that God wants us — and that he wants all of us!

Triumph of the Cross

Sharing in the Triumph of the Cross
John 3:13-17

How do we share in the triumph of the cross of Christ? We do so by accepting the cross in the same spirit with which Jesus accepted it: as a gift of love from the Father.

We are called to embrace the cross as an instrument of grace. When Moses lifted up the serpent in the desert, the Israelites were healed of their affliction. In an even more perfect manner, the lifting up of Jesus on the cross becomes the source of our eternal life. That is why the Church teaches that the human heart is converted by looking upon him whom our sins have pierced.

However, we cannot regard the cross as a detached bystander. Rather, Jesus commands: "Whoever wishes to come after me must deny himself, take up his cross, and follow me. . . . and whoever does not take up his cross and follow after me is not worthy of me" (Mt 16:24, 10:38). The triumph of the cross begins in us as we undertake the weight of the cross through penances that configure us to Christ and that allow us to become co-heirs with the risen Christ. This is possible because the cross of Christ has given new meaning to suffering.

When we esteem all our labors as a participation in the cross of Christ, we realize how human work serves as a means of sanctification by which earthly realities become animated with the Spirit of Christ. That is why we sign ourselves with the sign of the cross before our prayers and activities. The sign of the cross, as an instrument of grace, strengthens us in temptations and difficulties. And that is why the Church counsels us to examine our consciences before the Lord's cross.

Moreover, we are to unite ourselves to the cross as the altar of sacrifice and sanctification. "For God so loved the world that he gave his only Son, that who believes in him might not perish but might have eternal life." We profess our belief in Jesus by uniting ourselves to the perfect sacrifice Christ offered on the cross as a total offering to the Father's love. In this way, we make our lives a sacrifice to God.

Only by engaging in this worship do we share in the triumph of the cross. For the Church was born from the pierced heart of Christ hanging dead on the cross. The sacrifice of redemption offered by Jesus on the altar of the cross seals the law of human solidarity and charity. In fact, on the cross, Jesus' prayer and his gift of self are but one. That is why, in the Easter preface, the Church proclaims: "Christ showed himself to be the priest, the altar, and the lamb of sacrifice." To reverence the altar of the cross by our prayer and acts of sacrifice, we worship Christ himself.

And we are to venerate the cross as the throne of Christ. It is on the cross that Christ becomes King. It is through Christ's cross that the Kingdom of God will be definitively established. The Church prays, "God reigned from the wood."

Christ's death on the cross is our royal road to the exaltation of heaven. Jesus died lifted up so that we might raise our hearts to heavenly things. St. Rose of Lima reminds us: "Apart from the cross, there is no other ladder by which we may get to heaven."

The lifting up of Jesus on the cross signifies, announces, and begins his lifting up by his Ascension into heaven. That hope fills us with confidence as we genuflect and kiss the cross on Good Friday. The cruciform posture of the priest presiding at Mass reinforces the truth that underlies every prayer of the Church: "Hail, O cross, our only hope."

All Saints' Day

The Prevalence of Holiness
Matthew 5:1-12

Notice that when Jesus goes up on the mountainside to preach the Sermon on the Mount — Christ's manifesto of holiness — he doesn't take just a select group of his disciples. He doesn't take the cream of the crop, the elite, the most accomplished and gifted — the privileged chosen few showing the greatest potential. Rather, Jesus goes up to the mountain with "the crowds." As Christ makes his great proclamation of Gospel holiness, he declares that that holiness is offered to all.

As we celebrate the saints today, that is the first great truth which we profess: holiness in this life is possible. Holiness is within the reach of all. The littlest, the least talented, the most ill-equipped and unprepared have found a glorious place in heaven. We venerate saints of this sort in a special way because we see so much of ourselves in them. It is too easy for us to consider only the great and the powerful as candidates for sainthood and to relegate the yearning for holiness to them. Jesus calls us with the crowd to the summit of that mountain to impart to us the heights of holiness. All that is required for holiness is to be one with Jesus where he calls us and in the way that he calls us. He is the holiness that we become.

At the same time, the saints testify that human beings on their own apart from God cannot do anything good that makes them worthy of heaven. Christ himself makes us worthy of eternal life with God by enabling us to be good and to do good with God's own goodness. Sanctity becomes possible in our lives only once we relinquish any false notions of perfection and surrender ourselves to the goodness possible only in Jesus Christ.

Moreover, the Beatitudes convince us that holiness happens in a way that we would never expect. Christ's preaching reveals that true Christian holiness stands as a brazen contradiction to all our presuppositions. Sanctity belongs to those who are little. Happiness transforms those filled with sorrow. Elation elevates the lowly. The feast of love fills the famished. The joy of reconciliation suffuses the merciful. The ones who refuse to desire anything but what is pure are precisely the ones who embrace God with all their heart. Those who promote peace are most victorious. Those who are insulted and persecuted gain the greatest reward.

And holiness isn't something that happens only in heaven. The benefits of holiness begin now on earth in the experience of happiness. The genius of the Beatitudes is that they show us how powerfully the Father's merciful love is present and active in those very aspects of human life that otherwise make us most miserable.

Holiness is not some esoteric, mystic, cult-like striving for the divine. To be truly holy means to be fully human . . . alive with the life that Christ takes on and lays down and transforms for us so that we can be as holy as God. Holiness means committing ourselves to what Christ reveals in the Beatitudes. Beatitude means being one in love with Jesus. That is the communion that unites and delights the Communion of saints — that great "crowd" of the heavenly cloud who spend eternity interceding for us to join them in their joy.

ALL SOULS' DAY

THE GREATEST MOMENT OF LIFE: DEATH
John 6:37-40

In the earliest days of the Church, when Christians in Rome died, they wanted to be buried as near as possible to the grave of St. Peter. They believed that their closeness to the Vicar of Christ, even in death, would transform their death. By their union with the Church, these earliest Christians testified to the truth that, in death, "life is changed, not ended."

It is in that same spirit of hope-filled confidence and faith that the Church celebrates this ancient memorial of all the faithful departed. In an age of materialism, individualism, and instant gratification, the graces of this feast are needed more than ever.

For this feast poignantly reminds us that each day is a preparation for that most important moment of our lives: the moment of our death. As the Church prays in Eucharistic Prayer One, the undying witness of those who "have gone before us marked with the sign of faith" continues to form our growing faith by directing us to what really matters in life: to find in Christ's presence light, happiness, and peace.

Our dying began when we were born and baptized into Christ's death. This early, personal association with the saving death of Jesus gives Christians a supernatural approach to the reality of death that in turn characterizes their whole attitude toward life. With nearly every prayer, we remember that we are going to die: ". . . now and at the hour of our death." And that holy disposition toward mortality prepares and whets our appetite for the unending joy of eternal life.

However, it is only natural to have a fear of death. And the only way to overcome the fear of death is to die. Jesus says: "I came down from heaven not to do my own will but the will of the one who sent me." As the priest prays privately at Mass, "Lord Jesus Christ, by the will of the Father your death brought life to the world." Therefore, the Lord overcomes our fear of death by inviting us to embrace the will of the Father with him. It calls for a dying to self — expressed in self-forgetfulness and holy indifference.

The grace of indifference turns us away from our self-satisfaction with what we can understand and feel; it makes us yearn for the incomprehensible mysteries of heaven that lie beyond the limits of the human mind and senses. By this holy self-forgetfulness we refuse to set our hearts on anything but the Absolute — the infinite depths of God himself which we can encounter fully only by crossing from this life. Only that gives life meaning.

And then, in that spirit, all that the Father gives us shall come to us. And it will make us supremely happy, even if it means passing from earthly life. For as the Psalmist sings, "God's love is a greater good than life."

Jesus promises: "For this is the will of my Father, that everyone who sees the Son and believes in him may have eternal life." And as we see the Son in faith in the Eucharist, we know that, even now, we begin to possess and share in the eternal life which is our ultimate goal. As the Host is raised up, we are raised up. The holy souls encourage us: Resurrection begins now.

DEDICATION OF
ST. JOHN LATERAN BASILICA

THE CHURCH IS OUR MOTHER
John 2:13-22

Today's solemnity celebrates the dedication of the Lateran Basilica in Rome, the mother church of Roman Catholicism. As the inscription over the entrance of the building declares: "Mother and Head of all churches in the Holy City and throughout the World."

This solemnity reminds us how much we need the Church to be our Mother. For our meditation today brings to mind the truth that we have not given ourselves faith, just as we have not given ourselves life. That faith is mediated to us. We cannot believe without being supported by the faith of others. Our faith is engendered in us via the faith of our ancestors. The Lateran Basilica symbolizes that transmission and heritage.

In today's Gospel, Christ says to those who are selling doves: "Take these out of here, and stop making my Father's house a marketplace." The vendors violate the sanctity of the temple, and not simply through their crass commercialization which is greedy and exploitative. Rather, they defile the Holy Place through their profane disregard of the Holy One. They recognize all too readily how religion gives them a livelihood, but they totally ignore how God gives them life itself and calls them to live that life through obedient faith by seeking God above all things.

Today's solemnity checks similar temptations to individualism and self-seeking in ourselves. As we honor the mother of all churches, we rejoice in the supreme privilege of receiving the life of faith through the Church, our Mother. God has willed to make his people holy and to save them, but not as individuals. The Church, the Mother of our new birth, reveals how God sanctifies us precisely through that bond by which we become a people who profess God and who serve him in holiness.

As Christ drives out the animals from the temple area, "his disciples recalled the words of scripture: 'Zeal for your house will consume me.'" And this solemnity prompts a similar recollection in our minds. For the physical building of every church plays a crucial role in our life of faith. Churches are not simply gathering places. Rather, they are homes that direct our minds and hearts to our ultimate home in heaven.

To step into the house of God, we must be willing to leave behind the emptiness and evil of the world. That disposition is what distinguishes a pilgrim from a tourist in a church. As the Church teaches, the visible church is a symbol of the Father's house toward which the people of God is journeying. Crossing the threshold into that sacred building remains an act of faith before all else (it can even be a source of gaining indulgences). When that step is taken as a disciple, by entering into a church the Christian enters into the world of new Life it offers.

And finally, today's solemnity drives home that we are the Church. Visible churches make visible the people which is the Church living in this place. St. Gregory the Great reminds us that Christ has shown himself to be one Person with the holy Church he has taken to himself. As we contemplate this great basilica, as we gaze upon any church, we are poignantly reminded of our exalted vocation: Christ and his Church together make up the "whole Christ." As the Body of Christ, with profound humility, we receive the Body of Christ in church from Mother Church.

CONCLUSION
HOW TO LISTEN TO A HOMILY

What is the purpose of the Sunday homily? What are we supposed to "get out of it?" Perhaps one reason some preaching fails to impress us is that we are not sure how to listen to a homily. The Church charges priests with a very specific and well-focused goal every time they stand up to preach at Mass. The more we understand what the priest aims to accomplish in his preaching, the more we are given ears to hear the homily. The better equipped we are to listen well, the more do we become disposed to receive all the graces of the sacred encounter of preaching.

1. The homily enhances the faithful's participation in the Liturgy.

The Church teaches that Jesus Christ continues the work of our redemption in, with, and through the Church specifically through the liturgy. Every liturgical action remains a sacred action surpassing all others precisely because it is an action of Christ. This is especially true of preaching at Mass. Jesus Christ works in fullness for the transformation of all people in the sacraments, but especially in the Eucharist. Therefore, the chief goal of the homily is to lead us personally into the Sacrifice of Jesus Christ represented at Mass. The homily enables the faithful to enter more deeply into the liturgical celebration so as to understand and partake of the redemptive action of Christ made present there.

The homily is not meant to be commentary, instruction-giving, or even catechesis *per se*. Rather, the principal purpose of the homily is directed toward the liturgy itself and to a fuller participation in that liturgy. The homily seeks to unite us to the heavenly action that remains the source of all liturgy on earth.

A good homily will emphasize the saving actions of Jesus Christ represented liturgically, and will encourage us to partake of the graces those actions offer. The Church invites us to listen to the homily with a desire to celebrate the Eucharistic liturgy more fully, fervently, and faithfully. As we listen in this way, we realize that the homily leads, not to new ideas, but to deeper union with the Person of Christ himself. And that union saves us and transforms us. Therefore, it helps to listen to the homily by asking ourselves the question: *How does this homily lead me more deeply into the Paschal Mystery and all that that means?*

2. The homily provides a fitting way for the people of God to respond to God's Word.

At times, the real meaning of certain Scripture passages can elude us. Some figures of speech and particular literary devices may confuse us. We wonder what God's Word really means and how it applies to our daily life. And we know that taking a fundamentalistic approach to Sacred Scripture only makes matters worse.

However, the homily is a continuation of the proclamation of the Scriptures. In this way, that homily acts as a kind of translator or interpreter of the Word of God that gives the congregation ears to hear what God is speaking to them through his Word. The homily renders the deepest levels of meaning of Sacred Scripture accessible to believers. By clarifying what is obscure and confusing, good preaching unleashes the vibrancy and vitality of the Word of God so that the people of God can respond to it with similar fervor.

As a result, it remains very difficult for us to derive any benefit from the homily if we have not first listened attentively to the Word of God proclaimed. It is too easy for us to turn off Sacred Scripture when it comes across to us as obtuse, archaic, arcane, or even contradictory. At the same time, the preacher remains obliged to anticipate those aspects of the Scripture that may mystify or perplex us, and to address them in a fitting way in his homily. Therefore, to benefit from preaching, we must be willing to put our preconceptions, our impatience, and our skepticism on hold. Instead, as we listen to the homily we do well to ask: *What is God saying to me through his Word and how is he calling me to respond?*

3. The homily enables believers to articulate their faith.

Many of us have been in the position of finding ourselves lacking adequate words to express our faith despite our convicted belief. Also, at times Catholics get challenged to present the "biblical" foundation for doctrinal teachings. One integral objective of the Sunday is to provide for such legitimate needs.

The homily intends to supply the faithful with insights and explanations that enable them to articulate their faith. In this way, the homily helps us to recognize the far-reaching implications of the faith we already possess. A good homily provides light by which we see how our faith interacts with and informs all the realities of our human existence. We can find the sense in everything through faith.

Accordingly, a good homily demonstrates the practicality of the faith. It equips God's people to speak about the mysteries with clarity and cogency. It gives them concrete, sensible words that they can take away to make part of their daily personal evangelization. The homily enables Catholics to talk with confidence about what they believe.

As a result, the homily does not so much generate new faith as it deepens the believers' understanding of the very faith that draws them to the Eucharist in the first place. The homily engages that faith to actualize the Word of God in the minds and hearts of those who hear it at Mass. Thus, in listening to the homily, it profits us to ask: *How does the homily help me to understand my faith better so that I can communicate it better to those I meet?*

4. The homily fosters a unifying vision among the people of God.

When Catholics come to Mass, they bring with them all the many different ways they have of looking at things. These vast and varied perspectives are the result of countless different factors that make up our backgrounds: family, cultural conditions, socio-economic circumstances, education, age differences, ethnic influences, etc. And yet, it is the great hallmark of the Catholic Church that what unites us remains greater than any and all of the diversity in our life. That unifying power is what makes the Catholic Church catholic.

The homily is one of the Church's graced instruments of unity. For the homily gives focus to the many divergent and opposing points of view that accompany us to Mass. In this way the congregation can see the relevance and importance of the Sacred Scripture proclaimed. The homily gives us a Gospel way of looking at the world and looking at our life. It provides a vision of what it means to live by faith as a follower of Christ. It gives us eyes to see and appreciate the presence of God in everything. To see is to possess.

Therefore, in order to benefit from the homily, we must put aside our private world-views and obsessions, especially if they smack of prejudice, presumption, or narrow-mindedness. The homily is God's way of helping us to see ourselves as God sees us. The homily helps us to look into the Word of God so as to gain a new outlook on life. When we contemplate the blessings of faith through the vision of preaching, we are given a kind of foretaste of the beatific vision: the goal of our journey here below.

The unifying vision afforded by the homily helps us to see what the Word of God has to say to us, how it affects our life and transforms it. At the same time, Gospel preaching affirms the universality of the Gospel by showing how the Gospel appeals and applies to everyone without exception or discrimination. Thus, we might ask at Mass: *How does the homily help me see how God wants me to regard himself, the world, and my life?*

5. The homily helps to instill divine meaning in life.

"What could this homily possibly have to do with my life? What's in it for me?" Much preaching is dismissed with just these sentiments. When a homily comes across as too academic, speculative, abstract, and esoteric, it is no wonder that many zone out. However, to accuse a homily of "not being in touch with reality" requires that the accuser himself be in touch with reality. What is reality? What defines reality?

Facile, self-serving answers and easy, convenient solutions to life's problems have nothing to do with the Gospel of Jesus Christ. Those who presume that life should be an unending experience of comfort, leisure, indulgence, and convenience are the most out-of-touch folks imaginable. And yet, the way that many live betrays that this is how they define reality.

Every single human being struggles to find the meaning and the purpose of life. What the Gospel reveals is that the meaning of life is found precisely in the struggle. It is the role of the homily to speak to that struggle, to show us the presence and action of God in our afflictions, and to persuade us to see how Jesus offers us the grace of redemption in every experience of human life, especially our suffering. Because Jesus has redeemed every dimension of creation, Jesus can be discovered in every situation.

By virtue of the Redemption, Jesus has entered into and identified himself with every single human reality. Nothing human stands outside the purview and saving Providence of God. Christ has become the measure for assessing and interpreting our existence. To seek the meaning of "reality" without the light of Jesus Christ means to opt for the absurd and to doom oneself to futility.

Every good homily proclaims the preeminent relevance of the Gospel: Jesus Christ is in every circumstance. That is the Good News that transforms our otherwise meaningless lives. The homily acts to mediate the meaning that easily eludes our lives. The more we realize that Jesus is at the center of our lives, the more we see what's in the homily for us. Therefore, we allow the homily to do its job when we ask: *How does this homily help me to recognize the saving presence of Jesus Christ active in the practical concerns of my life?*

6. The homily evokes in Christians a life of ongoing prayer and worship.

One key goal of the homily is to engender in us a deeper spiritual life. What happens profoundly in the liturgy is to be carried away in the believer's heart so as to continue to nourish the soul through personal prayer.

God put us in the world to know, to love, and to serve him. Our life of constant prayer, praise, and thanksgiving insures that we fulfill our divine vocation, which in turn enables us to realize our human dignity and destiny.

Therefore, a good homily will form our understanding of prayer and our ability to pray. At the same time, the homily inspires us to desire to make a more perfect gift of ourselves to God. For, in a way, the homily itself is a kind of prayer that provides a model for our own life of prayer. Everything we think, desire, say, and do becomes a grateful expression of what we have first received from the Word of God.

In this way, preaching nourishes and fortifies our meditation. The Good News relayed via the homily augments our relationship with God. It leads us to listen to the homily by asking: *How does this homily help me to love God more and to live for him?*

7. The homily forms the faithful for mission.

The missionary nature of the Church is revealed in the act of preaching. The offer of salvation is meant to be proclaimed and shared. It goes out to all so that all might become the Body of Christ. The homily helps to form the members of the Church for Christian witness to the world. The new life we receive through God's saving Word isn't for ourselves alone. Like the multiplied loaves, it must be distributed to all the hungering so that they can have their fill.

Christians feed the world by their good example, which itself is formed by the Word of God. That all-powerful Word endows us with the grace to confront criticism, derision, confusion, and persecution. It blesses us with a godly conviction that overcomes all the antagonism, reticence, and reluctance of the world. The Church calls us to translate all the insight and assistance we have received from God's Word into life-giving actions that draw others into the same truth that has set us free.

A good homily makes it possible for us to do what the priest commands at the end of Mass: "Go in peace to love and serve the Lord." In other words, go forth to be bold, grace-filled instruments of the New Evangelization. The final question we might pose of the homily is: *How does this homily form and exhort me to be an evangelizer?*

We might conclude by reflecting on how this homiletic pattern of responding to the Word of God is embodied in the life of the Blessed Virgin Mary. The Word of God that Mary receives at the Immaculate Conception is ordered to nothing other than the glory of God and humanity's partaking of his divine life. The Annunciation presents the holy way for every Christian to respond to the grace of the Word of God. The Word of God that Mary articulates to her kinswoman at the Visitation fills Elizabeth with the joy of the Holy Spirit; even before the Word of God in Mary's womb can speak with a human voice, the faith-filled Mother of God announces his Gospel. When Jesus Christ is made visible at the Incarnation, the Christmas vision made possible through the maternity of Mary becomes the one that unites the world. The sorrowing Mother present at the cross of her Son testifies to the truth that the undying Word of God forever fills every misery and mystery of human existence with divine meaning. Mary's presence among the apostles at the Pentecost teaches them and us how to embrace the gift of the Spirit by cultivating a spiritual life fired by prayer. And Mary's Assumption proclaims to the world that the Word of God transforms and elevates every aspect of our human life. God relies on us, as he relies on Mary, to be beacons of the mercy of God with the whole of our body, soul, and spirit.

INDEX

Entries for such words such as "Christ," "Church," "God," etc., that appear on almost every page of the text are listed with the first page on which the word occurs followed by *"et passim."*

175